Beethoven Speaks

Beethoven Speaks

The Man and the Artist in His Own Words

Edited by Friedrich Kerst
and Henry Edward Krehbiel

WAKING LION PRESS

ISBN 978-1-4341-0352-9

Published by Waking Lion Press, an imprint of The Editorium

The Editorium, LLC
West Valley City, UT 84128-3917
wakinglionpress.com
wakinglion@editorium.com

Contents

Biographical Sketch

Ludwig van Beethoven (baptized 17 December 1770—26 March 1827) was a German composer and pianist. A crucial figure in the transition between the Classical and Romantic eras in Western art music, he remains one of the most famous and influential of all composers.

Background and early life

Beethoven was the grandson of a musician of Flemish origin named Ludwig van Beethoven (1712–73) who moved at the age of twenty to Bonn and was employed as a bass singer at the court of the Elector of Cologne, rising to become Kapellmeister (music director). Ludwig had one son, Johann van Beethoven (1740–1792), who worked as a tenor in the same musical establishment, also giving lessons on piano and violin to supplement his income. Johann married Maria Magdalena Keverich in 1767; she was the daughter of Johann Heinrich Keverich, who had been the head chef at the court of the Archbishopric of Trier.

Beethoven was born of this marriage in Bonn. There is no authentic record of the date of his birth; however, the registry of his baptism, in a Roman Catholic service at the Parish of St. Regius on 17 December 1770, survives. As children of that era were traditionally baptised the day after birth in the Catholic Rhine country, and it is known that Beethoven's family and his teacher Johann Albrechtsberger celebrated his birthday on 16 December, most scholars accept 16 December 1770 as Beethoven's date of birth. Of the seven children born to Johann van Beethoven, only Ludwig, the second-born, and two younger brothers survived infancy. Caspar Anton Carl was born on 8 April 1774, and Nikolaus Johann, the youngest, was born on 2 October 1776.

Beethoven's first music teacher was his father. Although tradition has it that Johann van Beethoven was a harsh instructor, and that the child Beethoven, "made to stand at the keyboard, was often in tears," the Grove Dictionary of Music and Musicians claimed that no solid documentation supported this, and asserted that "speculation and myth-making have both been productive." Beethoven had other local teachers: the court organist Gilles van den Eeden (d. 1782), Tobias Friedrich Pfeiffer (a family friend, who taught Beethoven the piano), and Franz Rovantini (a relative, who instructed him in playing the violin and viola). Beethoven's musical talent was obvious at a young age. Johann, aware of Leopold Mozart's successes in this area (with son Wolfgang and daughter Nannerl), attempted to exploit his son as a child prodigy, claiming that Beethoven was six (he was seven) on the posters for Beethoven's first public performance in March 1778.

Some time after 1779, Beethoven began his studies with his most important teacher in Bonn, Christian Gottlob Neefe, who was appointed the Court's Organist in that year. Neefe taught Beethoven composition, and by March 1783 had helped him write his first published composition: a set of keyboard variations (WoO 63). Beethoven soon began working with Neefe as assistant organist, at first unpaid (1781), and then as a paid employee (1784) of the court chapel conducted by the Kapellmeister Andrea Luchesi. His first three piano sonatas, named "Kurfürst" ("Elector") for their dedication to the Elector Maximilian Frederick (1708–1784), were published in 1783. Maximilian Frederick noticed Beethoven's talent early, and subsidised and encouraged the young man's musical studies.

Maximilian Frederick's successor as the Elector of Bonn was Maximilian Franz, the youngest son of Empress Maria Theresa of Austria, and he brought notable changes to Bonn. Echoing changes made in Vienna by his brother Joseph, he introduced reforms based on Enlightenment philosophy, with increased support for education and the arts. The teenage Beethoven was almost certainly influenced by these changes. He may also have been influenced at this time by ideas prominent in freemasonry, as Neefe and others around Beethoven were members of the local chapter of the Order of the Illuminati.

In March 1787 Beethoven traveled to Vienna (possibly at another's expense) for the first time, apparently in the hope of studying with Mozart. The details of their relationship are uncertain, including whether or not they actually met. After just two weeks Beethoven learned that his mother was severely ill, and returned home. His mother died shortly thereafter, and the father lapsed deeper into alcoholism. As a result, Beethoven became responsible for the care of his two younger brothers, and he spent the next five years in Bonn.

Beethoven was introduced to several people who became important in his life in these years. Franz Wegeler, a young medical student, introduced him to the von Breuning family (one of whose daughters Wegeler eventually married). Beethoven often visited the von Breuning household, where he taught piano to some of the children. Here he encountered German and classical literature. The von Breuning family environment was less stressful than his own, which was increasingly dominated by his father's decline. Beethoven also came to the attention of Count Ferdinand von Waldstein, who became a lifelong friend and financial supporter.

In 1789 Beethoven obtained a legal order by which half of his father's salary was paid directly to him for support of the family. He also contributed further to the family's income by playing viola in the court orchestra. This familiarised Beethoven with a variety of operas, including three by Mozart that were performed at court in this period. He also befriended Anton Reicha, a flautist and violinist of about his own age who was a nephew of the court orchestra's conductor, Josef Reicha.

Establishing his career in Vienna

Beethoven was probably first introduced to Joseph Haydn in late 1790, when the latter was traveling to London and stopped in Bonn around Christmas time. They met in Bonn on Haydn's return trip from London to Vienna in July 1792, and it is likely that arrangements were made at that time for Beethoven to study with the old master. With the Elector's help, Beethoven moved to Vienna in 1792. From 1790 to 1792, Beethoven composed a significant number of works (none were published at the time, and most are now listed as works without opus) that demonstrated his growing range and maturity. Musicologists identified a theme similar to those of his third symphony in a set of variations written in 1791. Beethoven left Bonn for Vienna in November 1792, amid rumors of war spilling out of France, and learned shortly after his arrival that his father had died. Count Waldstein in his farewell note to Beethoven wrote: "Through uninterrupted diligence you will receive Mozart's spirit through Haydn's hands." Over the next few years, Beethoven responded to the widespread feeling that he was a successor to the recently deceased Mozart by studying that master's work and writing works with a distinctly Mozartean flavor.

Beethoven did not immediately set out to establish himself as a composer, but rather devoted himself to study and performance. Working under Haydn's direction, he sought to master counterpoint. He also studied violin under Ignaz Schuppanzigh. Early in this period, he also began receiving occasional instruction from Antonio Salieri, primarily in Italian vocal composition style; this relationship persisted until at least 1802, and possibly 1809. With Haydn's departure for England in 1794, Beethoven was expected by the Elector to return home. He chose instead to remain in Vienna, continuing his instruction in counterpoint with Johann Albrechtsberger and other teachers. Although his stipend from the Elector expired, a number of Viennese noblemen had already recognised his ability and offered him financial support, among them Prince Joseph Franz Lobkowitz, Prince Karl Lichnowsky, and Baron Gottfried van Swieten.

By 1793, Beethoven established a reputation as an improviser in the salons of the nobility, often playing the preludes and fugues of J. S. Bach's Well-Tempered Clavier. His friend Nikolaus Simrock had begun publishing his compositions; the first are believed to be a set of variations (WoO 66). By 1793, he had established a reputation in Vienna as a piano virtuoso, but he apparently withheld works from publication so that their publication in 1795 would have greater impact. Beethoven's first public performance in Vienna was in March 1795, a concert in which he first performed one of his piano concertos. It is uncertain whether this was the First or Second. Documentary evidence is unclear, and both concertos were in a similar state of near-completion (neither was completed or published for several years). Shortly after this performance, he arranged for the publication of the first of his compositions to which he assigned an opus number, the three piano trios, Opus 1. These works were dedicated to his patron Prince Lichnowsky, and were a financial success; Beethoven's profits were nearly sufficient to cover his living expenses for a year.

Musical maturity

Beethoven composed his first six string quartets (Op. 18) between 1798 and 1800 (commissioned by, and dedicated to, Prince Lobkowitz). They were published in 1801. With premieres of his First and Second Symphonies in 1800 and 1803, Beethoven became regarded as one of the most important of a generation of young composers following Haydn and Mozart. He also continued to write in other forms, turning out widely known piano sonatas like the "Pathétique" sonata (Op. 13), which Cooper describes as "surpass[ing] any of his previous compositions, in strength of character, depth of emotion, level of originality, and ingenuity of motivic and tonal manipulation." He also completed his Septet (Op. 20) in 1799, which was one of his most popular works during his lifetime.

For the premiere of his First Symphony, Beethoven hired the Burgtheater on 2 April 1800, and staged an extensive program of music, including works by Haydn and Mozart, as well as his Septet, the First Symphony, and one of his piano concertos (the latter three works all then unpublished). The concert, which the Allgemeine musikalische Zeitung described as "the most interesting concert in a long time," was not without difficulties; among the criticisms was that "the players did not bother to pay any attention to the soloist."

Mozart and Haydn were undeniable influences. For example, Beethoven's quintet for piano and winds is said to bear a strong resemblance to Mozart's work for the same configuration, albeit with his own distinctive touches. But Beethoven's melodies, musical development, use of modulation and texture, and characterization of emotion all set him apart from his influences, and heightened the impact some of his early works made when they were first published. By the end of 1800 Beethoven and his music were already much in demand from patrons and publishers.

In May 1799, Beethoven taught piano to the daughters of Hungarian Countess Anna Brunsvik. During this time, Beethoven fell in love with the younger daughter Josephine who has therefore been identified as one of the more likely candidates for the addressee of his letter to the "Immortal Beloved" (in 1812). Shortly after these lessons, Josephine was married to Count Josef Deym. Beethoven was a regular visitor at their house, continuing to teach Josephine, and playing at parties and concerts. Her marriage was by all accounts happy (despite initial financial problems), and the couple had four children. Her relationship with Beethoven intensified after Deym died suddenly in 1804.

Beethoven had few other students. From 1801 to 1805, he tutored Ferdinand Ries, who went on to become a composer and later wrote Beethoven remembered, a book about their encounters. The young Carl Czerny studied with Beethoven from 1801 to 1803. Czerny went on to become a renowned music teacher himself, instructing Franz Liszt, and gave the Vienna premiere of Beethoven's fifth piano concerto (the "Emperor") in 1812.

Beethoven's compositions between 1800 and 1802 were dominated by two large-scale orchestral works, although he continued to produce other important works such as the piano sonata Sonata quasi una fantasia known as the "Moonlight Sonata." In the spring of 1801 he completed The Creatures of Prometheus, a ballet. The work received numerous performances in 1801 and 1802, and Beethoven rushed to publish a piano arrangement to capitalise on its early popularity. In the spring of 1802 he completed the Second Symphony, intended for performance at a concert that was canceled. The symphony received its premiere instead at a subscription concert in April 1803 at the Theater an der Wien, where Beethoven had been appointed composer in residence. In addition to the Second Symphony, the concert also featured the First Symphony, the Third Piano Concerto, and the oratorio

Christ on the Mount of Olives. Reviews were mixed, but the concert was a financial success; Beethoven was able to charge three times the cost of a typical concert ticket.

Beethoven's business dealings with publishers also began to improve in 1802 when his brother Carl, who had previously assisted him casually, began to assume a larger role in the management of his affairs. In addition to negotiating higher prices for recently composed works, Carl also began selling some of Beethoven's earlier unpublished works, and encouraged Beethoven (against the latter's preference) to also make arrangements and transcriptions of his more popular works for other instrument combinations. Beethoven acceded to these requests, as he could not prevent publishers from hiring others to do similar arrangements of his works.

Loss of hearing

Around 1796, by the age of 26, Beethoven began to lose his hearing. He suffered from a severe form of tinnitus, a "ringing" in his ears that made it hard for him to hear music; he also avoided conversation. The cause of Beethoven's deafness is unknown, but it has variously been attributed to typhus, auto-immune disorders (such as systemic lupus erythematosus), and even his habit of immersing his head in cold water to stay awake. The explanation from Beethoven's autopsy was that he had a "distended inner ear," which developed lesions over time.

As early as 1801, Beethoven wrote to friends describing his symptoms and the difficulties they caused in both professional and social settings (although it is likely some of his close friends were already aware of the problems). Beethoven, on the advice of his doctor, lived in the small Austrian town of Heiligenstadt, just outside Vienna, from April to October 1802 in an attempt to come to terms with his condition. There he wrote his Heiligenstadt Testament, a letter to his brothers which records his thoughts of suicide due to his growing deafness and records his resolution to continue living for and through his art. Over time, his hearing loss became profound: there is a well-attested story that, at the end of the premiere of his Ninth Symphony, he had to be turned around to see the tumultuous applause of the audience; hearing nothing, he wept. Beethoven's hearing loss did not prevent his composing music, but it made playing at concerts—a lucrative source of income—increasingly difficult. After a failed attempt in 1811 to perform his own Piano Concerto No. 5 (the "Emperor"), which was premiered by his student Carl Czerny, he never performed in public again.

A large collection of Beethoven's hearing aids, such as a special ear horn, can be viewed at the Beethoven House Museum in Bonn, Germany. Despite his obvious distress, Czerny remarked that Beethoven could still hear speech and music normally until 1812. By 1814 however, Beethoven was almost totally deaf, and when a group of visitors saw him play a loud arpeggio of thundering bass notes at his piano remarking, "Ist es nicht schön?" (Is it not beautiful?), they felt deep sympathy considering his courage and sense of humor (he lost the ability to hear higher frequencies first).

As a result of Beethoven's hearing loss, his conversation books are an unusually rich written resource. Used primarily in the last ten or so years of his life, his friends wrote in these books so that he could know what they were saying, and he then responded either orally or in the book. The books contain discussions about music and other matters, and give insights into Beethoven's thinking; they are a source for investigations into how he intended his music should be performed, and also his perception of his relationship to art. Out of a total of 400 conversation books, it has been suggested that 264 were destroyed (and others were altered) after Beethoven's death by Anton Schindler, who wished only an idealised biography of the composer to survive.

Patronage

While Beethoven earned income from publication of his works and from public performances, he also depended on the generosity of patrons for income, for whom he gave private performances and copies of works they commissioned for an exclusive period prior to their publication. Some of his early patrons, including Prince Lobkowitz and Prince Lichnowsky, gave him annual stipends in addition to commissioning works and purchasing published works.

Perhaps Beethoven's most important aristocratic patron was Archduke Rudolph, the youngest son of Emperor Leopold II, who in 1803 or 1804 began to study piano and composition with Beethoven. The cleric (Cardinal-Priest) and the composer became friends, and their meetings continued until 1824. Beethoven dedicated 14 compositions to Rudolph, including the Archduke Trio (1811) and his great Missa Solemnis (1823). Rudolph, in turn, dedicated one of his own compositions to Beethoven. The letters Beethoven wrote to Rudolph are today kept at the Gesellschaft der Musikfreunde in Vienna.

In the Autumn of 1808, after having been rejected for a position at the royal theatre, Beethoven received an offer from Napoleon's brother Jérôme Bonaparte, then king of Westphalia, for a well-paid position as

Kapellmeister at the court in Cassel. To persuade him to stay in Vienna, the Archduke Rudolph, Prince Kinsky and Prince Lobkowitz, after receiving representations from the composer's friends, pledged to pay Beethoven a pension of 4000 florins a year. Only Archduke Rudolph paid his share of the pension on the agreed date. Kinsky, immediately called to military duty, did not contribute and soon died after falling from his horse. Lobkowitz stopped paying in September 1811. No successors came forward to continue the patronage, and Beethoven relied mostly on selling composition rights and a small pension after 1815. The effects of these financial arrangements were undermined to some extent by war with France, which caused significant inflation when the government printed money to fund its war efforts.

The middle period

Beethoven's return to Vienna from Heiligenstadt was marked by a change in musical style, and is now designated as the start of his "Middle" or "Heroic" period. According to Carl Czerny, Beethoven said, "I am not satisfied with the work I have done so far. From now on I intend to take a new way." This "Heroic" phase was characterised by a large number of original works composed on a grand scale. The first major work employing this new style was the Third Symphony in E flat, known as the "Eroica." This work was longer and larger in scope than any previous symphony. When it premiered in early 1805 it received a mixed reception. Some listeners objected to its length or misunderstood its structure, while others viewed it as a masterpiece.

The "middle period" is sometimes associated with a "heroic" manner of composing, but the use of the term "heroic" has become increasingly controversial in Beethoven scholarship. The term is more frequently used as an alternative name for the middle period. The appropriateness of the term "heroic" to describe the whole middle period has been questioned as well: while some works, like the Third and Fifth Symphonies, are easy to describe as "heroic," many others, like the "Pastoral" Sixth Symphony, are not.

Some of the middle period works extend the musical language Beethoven had inherited from Haydn and Mozart. The middle period work includes the Third through Eighth Symphonies, the Rasumovsky, Harp and Serioso string quartets, the "Waldstein" and "Appassionata" piano sonatas, Christ on the Mount of Olives, the opera Fidelio, the Violin Concerto and many other compositions. During this time Beethoven's income came from publishing his works, from performances of them, and from his patrons. His position at the Theater an der Wien was terminated when the theater changed management in early 1804, and he was forced to move temporarily to the suburbs of Vienna with his friend Stephan von Breuning. This slowed work on Fidelio, his largest work to date, for a time. It was delayed again by the Austrian censor, and finally premiered in November 1805 to houses that were nearly empty because of the French occupation of the city. In addition to being a financial failure, this version of Fidelio was also a critical failure, and Beethoven began revising it.

During May 1809, when the attacking forces of Napoleon bombarded Vienna, according to Ferdinand Ries, Beethoven, very worried that the noise would destroy what remained of his hearing, hid in the basement of his brother's house, covering his ears with pillows.

The work of the middle period established Beethoven as a master. In a review from 1810, he was enshrined by E. T. A. Hoffmann as one of the three great "Romantic" composers; Hoffman called Beethoven's Fifth Symphony "one of the most important works of the age."

Personal and family difficulties

Beethoven's love life was hampered by class issues. In late 1801 he met a young countess, Julie ("Giulietta") Guicciardi through the Brunsvik family, at a time when he was giving regular piano lessons to Josephine Brunsvik. Beethoven mentions his love for Julie in a November 1801 letter to his boyhood friend, Franz Wegeler, but he could not consider marrying her, due to the class difference. Beethoven later dedicated to her his Sonata No. 14, now commonly known as the "Moonlight" Sonata.

His relationship with Josephine Brunsvik deepened after the death in 1804 of her aristocratic first husband, the Count Joseph Deym. Beethoven wrote Josephine 15 passionate love letters between late 1804 to around 1809/10. Although his feelings were obviously reciprocated, Josephine was forced by her family to withdraw from him in 1807. She cited her "duty" and the fact that she would have lost the custodianship of her aristocratic children had she remarried to a commoner. After Josephine married Baron von Stackelberg in 1810, Beethoven may have proposed unsuccessfully to Therese Malfatti, the supposed dedicatee of "Für Elise"; his status as a commoner may again have interfered with those plans.

In the spring of 1811 Beethoven became seriously ill, suffering headaches and high fever. On the advice of his doctor, he spent six weeks in the Bohemian spa town of Teplitz. The following winter, which was dominated by work on the Seventh symphony, he was again ill, and his doctor ordered him to spend the summer of 1812 at the spa Teplitz. It is certain that he was at Teplitz when he wrote a love letter to his "Immortal Beloved." The identity of the intended recipient has long been a subject of debate; candidates include Julie Guicciardi, Therese Malfatti, Josephine Brunsvik, and Antonie Brentano.

Beethoven visited his brother Johann at the end of October 1812. He wished to end Johann's cohabitation with Therese Obermayer, a woman who already had an illegitimate child. He was unable to convince Johann to end the relationship, and appealed to the local civic and religious authorities. Johann and Therese married on 9 November.

In early 1813 Beethoven apparently went through a difficult emotional period, and his compositional output dropped. His personal appearance degraded—it had generally been neat—as did his manners in public, especially when dining. Beethoven took care of his brother (who was suffering from tuberculosis) and his family, an expense that he claimed left him penniless.

Beethoven was finally motivated to begin significant composition again in June 1813, when news arrived of the defeat of one of Napoleon's armies at Vitoria, Spain, by a coalition of forces under the Duke of Wellington. This news stimulated him to write the battle symphony known as Wellington's Victory. It was first performed on 8 December, along with his Seventh Symphony, at a charity concert for victims of the war. The work was a popular hit, probably because of its programmatic style that was entertaining and easy to understand. It received repeat performances at concerts Beethoven staged in January and February 1814. Beethoven's renewed popularity led to demands for a revival of Fidelio, which, in its third revised version, was also well-received at its July opening. That summer he composed a piano sonata for the first time in five years (No. 27, Opus 90). This work was in a markedly more Romantic style than his earlier sonatas. He was also one of many composers who produced music in a patriotic vein to entertain the many heads of state and diplomats that came to the Congress of Vienna that began in November 1814. His output of songs included his only song cycle, "An die ferne Geliebte," and the extraordinarily expressive second setting of the poem "An die Hoffnung" (Op. 94) in 1815. Compared to its first setting in 1805 (a gift for Josephine Brunsvik), it was "far more dramatic . . . The entire spirit is that of an operatic scena."

Custody struggle and illness

Between 1815 and 1817 Beethoven's output dropped again. Beethoven attributed part of this to a lengthy illness (he called it an "inflammatory fever") that afflicted him for more than a year, starting in October 1816. Biographers have speculated on a variety of other reasons that also contributed to the decline, including the difficulties in the personal lives of his would-be paramours and the harsh censorship policies of the Austrian government. The illness and death of his brother Carl from consumption may also have played a role.

Carl had been ill for some time, and Beethoven spent a small fortune in 1815 on his care. After Carl died on 15 November 1815, Beethoven immediately became embroiled in a protracted legal dispute with Carl's wife Johanna over custody of their son Karl, then nine years old. Beethoven, who considered Johanna an unfit parent because of her morals (she had an illegitimate child by a different father before marrying Carl, and had been convicted of theft) and financial management, had successfully applied to Carl to have himself named sole guardian of the boy. A late codicil to Carl's will gave him and Johanna joint guardianship. While Beethoven was successful at having his nephew removed from her custody in February 1816, the case was not fully resolved until 1820, and he was frequently preoccupied by the demands of the litigation and seeing to Karl's welfare, whom he first placed in a private school.

The Austrian court system had one court for the nobility and members of the Landtafel, the R&I Landrechte, and many other courts for commoners, among them the Civil Court of the Vienna Magistrate. Beethoven disguised the fact that the Dutch "van" in his name did not denote nobility as does the German "von" and his case was tried in the Landrechte. Owing to his influence with the court, Beethoven felt assured of the favorable outcome of being awarded sole guardianship. While giving evidence to the Landrechte, however, Beethoven inadvertently admitted that he was not nobly born. The case was transferred to the Magistracy on 18 December 1818, where he lost sole guardianship.

Beethoven appealed, and regained custody. Johanna's appeal to the Emperor was not successful: the Emperor "washed his hands of the matter." During the years of custody that followed, Beethoven attempted to ensure that Karl lived to the highest moral standards. Beethoven had an overbearing manner and frequently interfered in his nephew's life. Karl attempted suicide on 31 July 1826 by shooting himself in the head. He survived, and was brought to his mother's house, where he recuperated. He and Beethoven were reconciled, but Karl insisted on joining the army, and last saw Beethoven in early 1827.

The only major works Beethoven produced during this time were two cello sonatas, a piano sonata, and collections of folk song settings.

Late works

Beethoven began a renewed study of older music, including works by J. S. Bach and Handel, that were then being published in the first attempts at complete editions. He composed the Consecration of the House Overture, which was the first work to attempt to incorporate these influences. A new style emerged, now called his "Late period." He returned to the keyboard to compose his first piano sonatas in almost a decade: the works of the Late period are commonly held to include the last five piano sonatas and the Diabelli Variations, the last two sonatas for cello and piano, the late string quartets (see below), and two works for very large forces: the Missa Solemnis and the Ninth Symphony.

By early 1818 Beethoven's health had improved, and his nephew moved in with him in January. On the downside, his hearing had deteriorated to the point that conversation became difficult, necessitating the use of conversation books. His household management had also improved somewhat; Nanette Streicher, who had assisted in his care during his illness, continued to provide some support, and he finally found a skilled cook. His musical output in 1818 was still somewhat reduced, but included song collections and the Hammerklavier Sonata, as well as sketches for two symphonies that eventually coalesced into the epic Ninth. In 1819 he was again preoccupied by the legal processes around Karl, and began work on the Diabelli Variations and the Missa Solemnis.

For the next few years he continued to work on the Missa, composing piano sonatas and bagatelles to satisfy the demands of publishers and the need for income, and completing the Diabelli Variations. He was ill again for an extended time in 1821, and completed the Missa in 1823, three years after its original due date. He also opened discussions with his publishers over the possibility of producing a complete edition of his work, an idea that was arguably not fully realised until 1971. Beethoven's brother Johann began to take a hand in his business affairs, much in the way Carl had earlier, locating older unpublished works to offer for publication and offering the Missa to multiple publishers with the goal of getting a higher price for it.

Two commissions in 1822 improved Beethoven's financial prospects. The Philharmonic Society of London offered a commission for a symphony, and Prince Nikolay Golitsin of St. Petersburg offered to pay Beethoven's price for three string quartets. The first of these commissions spurred Beethoven to finish the Ninth Symphony, which was first performed, along with the Missa Solemnis, on 7 May 1824, to great acclaim at the Kärntnertortheater. The Allgemeine musikalische

Zeitung gushed, "inexhaustible genius had shown us a new world," and Carl Czerny wrote that his symphony "breathes such a fresh, lively, indeed youthful spirit . . . so much power, innovation, and beauty as ever [came] from the head of this original man, although he certainly sometimes led the old wigs to shake their heads." Unlike his more lucrative earlier concerts, this did not make Beethoven much money, as the expenses of mounting it were significantly higher. A second concert on 24 May, in which the producer guaranteed Beethoven a minimum fee, was poorly attended; nephew Karl noted that "many people have already gone into the country." It was Beethoven's last public concert.

Beethoven then turned to writing the string quartets for Golitsin. This series of quartets, known as the "Late Quartets," went far beyond what musicians or audiences were ready for at that time. One musician commented that "we know there is something there, but we do not know what it is." Composer Louis Spohr called them "indecipherable, uncorrected horrors." Opinion has changed considerably from the time of their first bewildered reception: their forms and ideas inspired musicians and composers including Richard Wagner and Béla Bartók, and continue to do so. Of the late quartets, Beethoven's favorite was the Fourteenth Quartet, op. 131 in C# minor, which he rated as his most perfect single work. The last musical wish of Schubert was to hear the Op. 131 quartet, which he did on 14 November 1828, five days before his death.

Beethoven wrote the last quartets amidst failing health. In April 1825 he was bedridden, and remained ill for about a month. The illness—or more precisely, his recovery from it—is remembered for having given rise to the deeply felt slow movement of the Fifteenth Quartet, which Beethoven called "Holy song of thanks ('Heiliger dankgesang') to the divinity, from one made well." He went on to complete the quartets now numbered Thirteenth, Fourteenth, and Sixteenth. The last work completed by Beethoven was the substitute final movement of the Thirteenth Quartet, which replaced the difficult Große Fuge. Shortly thereafter, in December 1826, illness struck again, with episodes of vomiting and diarrhea that nearly ended his life.

Illness and death

Beethoven was bedridden for most of his remaining months, and many friends came to visit. Beethoven died on 26 March 1827 at the age of 56 during a thunderstorm. His friend Anselm Hüttenbrenner, who was present at the time, claimed that there was a peal of thunder at the moment of death. An autopsy revealed significant liver damage, which may have been due to heavy alcohol consumption. It also revealed considerable dilation of the auditory and other related nerves.

Beethoven's funeral procession on 29 March 1827 was attended by an estimated 20,000 Viennese citizens. Franz Schubert, who died the following year and was buried next to Beethoven, was one of the torch-bearers. Unlike Mozart, who was buried anonymously in a communal grave (the custom at the time), Beethoven was buried in a dedicated grave in the Währing cemetery, north-west of Vienna, after a requiem mass at the church of the Holy Trinity (Dreifaltigkeitskirche). His remains were exhumed for study in 1862, and moved in 1888 to Vienna's Zentralfriedhof.

There is dispute about the cause of Beethoven's death: alcoholic cirrhosis, syphilis, infectious hepatitis, lead poisoning, sarcoidosis, and Whipple's disease have all been proposed. Friends and visitors before and after his death clipped locks of his hair, some of which have been preserved and subjected to additional analysis, as have skull fragments removed during the 1862 exhumation. Some of these analyses have led to controversial assertions that Beethoven was accidentally poisoned to death by excessive doses of lead-based treatments administered under instruction from his doctor.

Character

Beethoven's personal life was troubled by his encroaching deafness and irritability brought on by chronic abdominal pain (beginning in his twenties) which led him to contemplate suicide (documented in his Heiligenstadt Testament). Beethoven was often irascible. It has been suggested he suffered from bipolar disorder. Nevertheless, he had a close and devoted circle of friends all his life, thought to have been attracted by his strength of personality. Toward the end of his life, Beethoven's friends competed in their efforts to help him cope with his incapacities.

Sources show Beethoven's disdain for authority, and for social rank. He stopped performing at the piano if the audience chatted amongst themselves, or afforded him less than their full attention. At soirées, he refused to perform if suddenly called upon to do so. Eventually, after many confrontations, the Archduke Rudolph decreed that the usual rules of court etiquette did not apply to Beethoven.

Beethoven was attracted to the ideals of the Enlightenment. In 1804, when Napoleon's imperial ambitions became clear, Beethoven took hold of the title-page of his Third Symphony and scratched the name

Bonaparte out so violently that he made a hole in the paper. He later changed the work's title to "Sinfonia Eroica, composta per festeggiare il sovvenire d'un grand'uom" ("Heroic Symphony, composed to celebrate the memory of a great man"), and he rededicated it to his patron, Prince Joseph Franz von Lobkowitz, at whose palace it was first performed.

The fourth movement of his Ninth Symphony features an elaborate choral setting of Schiller's Ode An die Freude ("Ode to Joy"), an optimistic hymn championing the brotherhood of humanity.

Music

Beethoven is acknowledged as one of the giants of classical music; occasionally he is referred to as one of the "three Bs" (along with Bach and Brahms) who epitomise that tradition. He was also a pivotal figure in the transition from the 18th century musical classicism to 19th century romanticism, and his influence on subsequent generations of composers was profound.

Beethoven composed in several musical genres and for a variety of instrument combinations. His works for symphony orchestra include nine symphonies (the Ninth Symphony includes a chorus), and about a dozen pieces of "occasional" music. He wrote seven concerti for one or more soloists and orchestra, as well as four shorter works that include soloists accompanied by orchestra. His only opera is Fidelio; other vocal works with orchestral accompaniment include two masses and a number of shorter works.

His large body of compositions for piano includes 32 piano sonatas and numerous shorter pieces, including arrangements of some of his other works. Works with piano accompaniment include 10 violin sonatas, 5 cello sonatas, and a sonata for French horn, as well as numerous lieder.

Beethoven also wrote a significant quantity of chamber music. In addition to 16 string quartets, he wrote five works for string quintet, seven for piano trio, five for string trio, and more than a dozen works for various combinations of wind instruments.

Preface

This little book came into existence as if it were by chance. The author had devoted himself for a long time to the study of Beethoven and carefully scrutinized all manner of books, publications, manuscripts, etc., in order to derive the greatest possible information about the hero. He can say confidently that he conned every existing publication of value. His notes made during his readings grew voluminous, and also his amazement at the wealth of Beethoven's observations comparatively unknown to his admirers because hidden away, like concealed violets, in books which have been long out of print and for whose reproduction there is no urgent call. These observations are of the utmost importance for the understanding of Beethoven, in whom man and artist are inseparably united. Within the pages of this little book are included all of them which seemed to possess value, either as expressions of universal truths or as evidence of the character of Beethoven or his compositions. Beethoven is brought more directly before our knowledge by these his own words than by the diffuse books which have been written about him. For this reason the compiler has added only the necessary explanatory notes, and (on the advice of professional friends) the remarks introductory to the various subdivisions of the book. He dispensed with a biographical introduction; there are plenty of succinct biographies, which set forth the circumstances of the master's life easily to be had. Those who wish to penetrate farther into the subject would do well to read the great work by Thayer, the foundation of all Beethoven biography (in the new revision now making by Deiters), or the critical biography by Marx, as revised by Behncke. In sifting the material it was found that it fell naturally into thirteen subdivisions. In arranging the succession of utterances care was had to group related subjects. By this means unnecessary interruptions in the train of thought were avoided and interesting comparisons made possible. To this end it was important that time, place and circumstances of every word should be conscientiously set down.

Concerning the selection of material let it be said that in all cases of doubt the authenticity of every utterance was proved; Beethoven is easily recognizable in the form and contents of his sayings. Attention must be directed to two matters in particular: after considerable reflection the compiler decided to include in the collection a few quotations which Beethoven copied from books which he read. From the fact that he took the trouble to write them down, we may assume that they had a fascination for him, and were greeted with lively emotion as being admirable expressions of thoughts which had moved him. They are very few, and the fact that they are quotations is plainly indicated. By copying them into his note-books Beethoven as much as stored them away in the thesaurus of his thoughts, and so they may well have a place here. A word touching the use of the three famous letters to Bettina von Arnim, the peculiarities of which differentiate them from the entire mass of Beethoven's correspondence and compel an inquiry into their genuineness: As a correspondent Bettina von Arnim has a poor reputation since the discovery of her pretty forgery, "Goethes Briefwechsel mit einem Kinde" (Goethe's Correspondence with a Child). In this alleged "Correspondence" she made use of fragmentary material which was genuine, pieced it out with her own inventions, and even went so far as to turn into letters poems written by Goethe to her and other women. The genuineness of a poem by Beethoven to Bettina is indubitable; it will be found in the chapter entitled "Concerning Texts." Doubt was thrown on the letters immediately on their appearance in 1839.

Bettina could have dissipated all suspicion had she produced the originals and remained silent. One letter, however, that dated February 10, 1811, afterward came to light. Bettina had given it to Philipp von Nathusius. It had always been thought the most likely one, of the set to be authentic; the compiler has therefore, used it without hesitation. From the other letters, in which a mixture of the genuine and the fictitious must be assumed so long as the originals are not produced, passages have been taken which might have been thus constructed by Beethoven. On the contrary, the voluminous communications of Bettina to Goethe, in which she relates her conversations with Beethoven, were scarcely used. It is significant, so far as these are concerned, that, according to Bettina's own statement, when she read the letter to him before sending it off, Beethoven cried out, "Did I really say that? If so I must have had a raptus."

In conclusion the compiler directs attention to the fact that in a few cases utterances which have been transmitted to us only in an indirect form have been altered to present them in a direct form, in as much as their contents seemed too valuable to omit simply because their production involved a trifling change in form.

—Elberfeld, October, 1904. Fr. K.

Chapter 1

On Art

Beethoven's relation to art might almost be described as personal. Art was his goddess to whom he made petition, to whom he rendered thanks, whom he defended. He praised her as his savior in times of despair; by his own confession it was only the prospect of her comforts that prevented him from laying violent hands on himself. Read his words and you shall find that it was his art that was his companion in his wanderings through field and forest, the sharer of the solitude to which his deafness condemned him. The concepts Nature and Art were intimately bound up in his mind. His lofty and idealistic conception of art led him to proclaim the purity of his goddess with the hot zeal of a priestly fanatic. Every form of pseudo or bastard art stirred him with hatred to the bottom of his soul; hence his furious onslaughts on mere virtuosity and all efforts from influential sources to utilize art for other than purely artistic purposes. And his art rewarded his devotion richly; she made his sorrowful life worth living with gifts of purest joy:

"To Beethoven music was not only a manifestation of the beautiful, an art, it was akin to religion. He felt himself to be a prophet, a seer. All the misanthropy engendered by his unhappy relations with mankind, could not shake his devotion to this ideal which had sprung in to Beethoven from truest artistic apprehension and been nurtured by enforced introspection and philosophic reflection."

("Music and Manners," page 237. H. E. K.)

1. "'Tis said, that art is long, and life but fleeting:—Nay; life is long, and brief the span of art; If e're her breath vouchsafes with gods a meeting, A moment's favor 'tis of which we've had a part."

(Conversation-book, March, 1820. Probably a quotation.)

2. "The world is a king, and, like a king, desires flattery in return for favor; but true art is selfish and perverse—it will not submit to the mould of flattery."

(Conversation-book, March, 1820. When Baron van Braun expressed the opinion that the opera "Fidelio" would eventually win the enthusiasm of the upper tiers, Beethoven said, "I do not write for the galleries!" He never permitted himself to be persuaded to make concessions to the taste of the masses.)

3. "Continue to translate yourself to the heaven of art; there is no more undisturbed, unmixed, purer happiness than may thus be attained."

(August 19, 1817, to Xavier Schnyder, who vainly sought instruction from Beethoven in 1811, though he was pleasantly received.)

4. "Go on; do not practice art alone but penetrate to her heart; she deserves it, for art and science only can raise man to godhood."

(Teplitz, July 17, 1812, to his ten years' old admirer, Emilie M. in H.)

5. "True art is imperishable and the true artist finds profound delight in grand productions of genius."

(March 15, 1823, to Cherubini, to whom he also wrote, "I prize your works more than all others written for the stage." The letter asked Cherubini to interest himself in obtaining a subscription from King Louis XVIII for the Solemn Mass in D).

[Cherubini declared that he had never received the letter. That it was not only the hope of obtaining a favor which prompted Beethoven to express so high an admiration for Cherubini, is plain from a remark made by the English musician Cipriani Potter to A. W. Thayer in 1861. I found it in Thayer's note-books which were placed in my hands for examination after his death.

One day Potter asked, "Who is the greatest living composer, yourself excepted?" Beethoven seemed puzzled for a moment, and then exclaimed, "Cherubini." H. E. K.]

6. "Truth exists for the wise; beauty for the susceptible heart. They belong together—are complementary."

(Written in the autograph book of his friend, Lenz von Breuning, in 1797.)

7. "When I open my eyes, a sigh involuntarily escapes me, for all that I see runs counter to my religion; perforce I despise the world which does not intuitively feel that music is a higher revelation than all wisdom and philosophy."

(Remark made to Bettina von Arnim, in 1810, concerning Viennese society. Report in a letter by Bettina to Goethe on May 28, 1810.)

8. "Art! Who comprehends her? With whom can one consult concerning this great goddess?"

(August 11, 1810, to Bettina von Arnim.)

9. "In the country I know no lovelier delight than quartet music."

(To Archduke Rudolph, in a letter addressed to Baden on July 24, 1813.)

10. "Nothing but art, cut to form like old-fashioned hoop-skirts. I never feel entirely well except when I am among scenes of unspoiled nature."

(September 24, 1826, to Breuning, while promenading with Breuning's family in the Schonbrunner Garden, after calling attention to the alleys of trees "trimmed like walls, in the French manner.")

11. "Nature knows no quiescence; and true art walks with her hand in hand; her sister—from whom heaven forefend us!—is called artificiality."

(From notes in the lesson book of Archduke Rudolph, following some remarks on the expansion of the expressive capacity of music.)

Chapter 2

On Nature

Beethoven was a true son of the Rhine in his love for nature. As a boy he had taken extended trips, sometimes occupying days, with his father "through the Rhenish localities ever lastingly dear to me." In his days of physical health Nature was his instructress in art; "I may not come without my banner," he used to say when he set out upon his wanderings even in his latest years, and never without his note books. In the scenes of nature he found his marvelous motives and themes; brook, birds and tree sang to him. In a few special cases he has himself recorded the fact.

But when he was excluded more and more from communion with his fellow men because of his increasing deafness, until, finally, he could communicate only by writing with others (hence the conversation-books, which will be cited often in this little volume), he fled for refuge to nature. Out in the woods he again became naively happy; to him the woods were a Holy of Holies, a Home of the Mysteries. Forest and mountain-vale heard his sighs; there he unburdened his heavy-laden heart. When his friends need comfort he recommends a retreat to nature. Nearly every summer he leaves hot and dusty Vienna and seeks a quiet spot in the beautiful neighborhood. To call a retired and reposeful little spot his own is his burning desire.

12. On the Kahlenberg, 1812, end of September:
Almighty One In the woods I am blessed. Happy every one In the woods. Every tree speaks Through Thee.

O God! What glory in the Woodland. On the Heights is Peace,—Peace to serve Him—

(This poetic exclamation, accompanied by a few notes, is on a page of music paper owned by Joseph Joachim.)

13. "How happy I am to be able to wander among bushes and herbs, under trees and over rocks; no man can love the country as I love it. Woods, trees and rocks send back the echo that man desires."

(To Baroness von Drossdick.)

14. "O God! send your glance into beautiful nature and comfort your moody thoughts touching that which must be."

(To the "Immortal Beloved," July 6, in the morning.)

[Thayer has spoiled the story so long believed, and still spooking in the books of careless writers, that the "Immortal Beloved" was the Countess Giulietta Guicciardi, to whom the C-sharp minor sonata is dedicated. The real person to whom the love-letters were addressed was the Countess Brunswick to whom Beethoven was engaged to be married when he composed the fourth Symphony. H. E. K.)

15. "My miserable hearing does not trouble me here. In the country it seems as if every tree said to me: 'Holy! holy!' Who can give complete expression to the ecstasy of the woods! O, the sweet stillness of the woods!"

(July, 1814; he had gone to Baden after the benefit performance of "Fidelio.")

16. "My fatherland, the beautiful locality in which I saw the light of the world, appears before me vividly and just as beautiful as when I left you; I shall count it the happiest experience of my life when I shall again be able to see you, and greet our Father Rhine."

(Vienna, June 29, to Wegeler, in Bonn.)

[In 1825 Beethoven said to his pupil Ries, "Fare well in the Rhine country which is ever dear to me," and in 1826 wrote to Schott, the publisher in Mayence, about the "Rhine country which I so long to see again."]

17. "Bruhl, at "The Lamb"—how lovely to see my native country again!"

(Diary, 1812–1818.)

18. "A little house here, so small as to yield one's self a little room,— only a few days in this divine Bruehl,—longing or desire, emancipation or fulfillment."

(Written in 1816 in Bruehl near Modling among the sketches for the Scherzo of the pianoforte sonata op. 10.)

[Like many another ejaculatory remark of Beethoven's, it is difficult to understand. See Appendix. H. E. K.]

19. "When you reach the old ruins, think that Beethoven often paused there; if you wander through the mysterious fir forests, think that Beethoven often poetized, or, as is said, composed there."

(In the fall of 1817, to Mme. Streicher, who was at a cure in Baden.)

20. "Nature is a glorious school for the heart! It is well; I shall be a scholar in this school and bring an eager heart to her instruction. Here I shall learn wisdom, the only wisdom that is free from disgust; here

I shall learn to know God and find a foretaste of heaven in His knowledge. Among these occupations my earthly days shall flow peacefully along until I am accepted into that world where I shall no longer be a student, but a knower of wisdom."

(Copied into his diary, in 1818, from Sturm's "Betrachtungen uber die Werke Gottes in der Natur.")

21. "Soon autumn will be here. Then I wish to be like unto a fruitful tree which pours rich stores of fruit into our laps! But in the winter of existence, when I shall be gray and sated with life, I desire for myself the good fortune that my repose be as honorable and beneficent as the repose of nature in the winter time."

(Copied from the same work of Sturm's.)

Chapter 3

On Texts

Not even a Beethoven was spared the tormenting question of texts for composition. It is fortunate for posterity that he did not exhaust his energies in setting inefficient libretti, that he did not believe that good music would suffice to command success in spite of bad texts. The majority of his works belong to the field of purely instrumental music. Beethoven often gave expression to the belief that words were a less capable medium of proclamation for feelings than music. Nevertheless it may be observed that he looked upon an opera, or lyric drama, as the crowning work of his life. He was in communication with the best poets of his time concerning opera texts. A letter of his on the subject was found in the blood-spotted pocketbook of Theodor Komer. The conclusion of his creative labors was to be a setting of Goethe's "Faust;" except "Fidelio," however, he gave us no opera. His songs are not many although he sought carefully for appropriate texts. Unhappily the gift of poetry was not vouchsafed him.

22. "Always the same old story: the Germans can not put together a good libretto."

(To C. M. von Weber, concerning the book of "Euryanthe," at Baden, in October, 1823. Mozart said: "Verses are the most indispensable thing for music, but rhymes, for the sake of rhymes, the most injurious. Those who go to work so pedantically will assuredly come to grief, along with the music.")

23. "It is difficult to find a good poem. Grillparzer has promised to write one for me,—indeed, he has already written one; but we can not understand each other. I want something entirely different than he."

(In the spring of 1825, to Ludwig Rellstab, who was intending to write an opera-book for Beethoven. It may not be amiss to recall the fact that Mozart examined over one hundred librettos, according to his own statement, before he decided to compose "The Marriage of Figaro.")

7

24. "It is the duty of every composer to be familiar with all poets, old and new, and himself choose the best and most fitting for his purposes."

(In a recommendation of Kandler's "Anthology.")

25. "The genre would give me little concern provided the subject were attractive to me. It must be such that I can go to work on it with love and ardor. I could not compose operas like 'Don Juan' and 'Figaro;' toward them I feel too great a repugnance. I could never have chosen such subjects; they are too frivolous."

(In the spring of 1825, to Ludwig Rellstab.)

26. "I need a text which stimulates me; it must be something moral, uplifting. Texts such as Mozart composed I should never have been able to set to music. I could never have got myself into a mood for licentious texts. I have received many librettos, but, as I have said, none that met my wishes."

(To young Gerhard von Breuning.)

27. "I know the text is extremely bad, but after one has conceived an entity out of even a bad text, it is difficult to make changes in details without disturbing the unity. If it is a single word, on which occasionally great weight is laid, it must be permitted to stand. He is a bad author who can not, or will not try to make something as good as possible; if this is not the case petty changes will certainly not improve the whole."

(Teplitz, August 23, 1811, to Hartel, the publisher, who wanted some changes made in the hook of "The Mount of Olives.")

28. "Good heavens! Do they think in Saxony that the words make good music? If an inappropriate word can spoil the music, which is true, then we ought to be glad when we find that words and music are one and not try to improve matters even if the verbal expression is commonplace—dixi."

(January 28, to Gottfried Hartel, who had undertaken to make changes in the book of "The Mount of Olives" despite the prohibition of Beethoven.)

29. "Goethe's poems exert a great power over me not only because of their contents but also because of their rhythms; I am stimulated to compose by this language, which builds itself up to higher orders as if through spiritual agencies, and bears in itself the secret of harmonies."

(Reported as an expression of Beethoven's by Bettina von Arnim to Goethe.)

30. "Schiller's poems are difficult to set to music. The composer must be able to rise far above the poet. Who can do that in the case of Schiller? In this respect Goethe is much easier."

(1809, after Beethoven had made his experiences with the "Hymn to Joy" and "Egmont.")

Chapter 4

On Composing

Wiseacres not infrequently accused Beethoven of want of regularity in his compositions. In various ways and at divers times he gave vigorous utterance to his opinions of such pedantry. He was not the most tractable of pupils, especially in Vienna, where, although he was highly praised as a player, he took lessons in counterpoint from Albrechtsberger. He did not endure long with Papa Haydn. He detested the study of fugue in particular; the fugue was to him a symbol of narrow coercion which choked all emotion. Mere formal beauty, moreover, was nothing to him. Over and over again he emphasizes soul, feeling, direct and immediate life, as the first necessity of an art work. It is therefore not strange that under certain circumstances he ignored conventional forms in sonata and symphony. An irrepressible impulse toward freedom is the most prominent peculiarity of the man and artist Beethoven; nearly all of his observations, no matter what their subject, radiate the word "Liberty." In his remarks about composing there is a complete exposition of his method of work.

31. "As regards me, great heavens! my dominion is in the air; the tones whirl like the wind, and often there is a like whirl in my soul."
(February 13, 1814, to Count Brunswick, in Buda.)

32. "Then the loveliest themes slipped out of your eyes into my heart, themes which shall only then delight the world when Beethoven conducts no longer."
(August 15, 1812, to Bettina von Arnim.)

33. "I always have a picture in my mind when composing, and follow its lines."
(In 1815, to Neate, while promenading with him in Baden and talking about the "Pastoral" symphony.)

[Ries relates: "While composing Beethoven frequently thought of an object, although he often laughed at musical delineation and scolded about petty things of the sort. In this respect 'The Creation' and 'The Seasons' were many times a butt, though without depreciation of Haydn's loftier merits. Haydn's choruses and other works were loudly praised by Beethoven."]

34. "The texts which you sent me are least of all fitted for song. The description of a picture belongs to the field of painting; in this the poet can count himself more fortunate than my muse for his territory is not so restricted as mine in this respect, though mine, on the other hand, extends into other regions, and my dominion is not easily reached."

(Nussdorf, July 15, 1817, to Wilhelm Gerhard, who had sent him some Anacreontic songs for composition.)

35. "Carried too far, all delineation in instrumental music loses in efficiency."

(A remark in the sketches for the "Pastoral" symphony, preserved in the Royal Library in Berlin.)

[Mozart said: "Even in the most terrifying moments music must never offend the ear."]

36. "Yes, yes, then they are amazed and put their heads together because they never found it in any book on thorough bass."

(To Ries when the critics accused him of making grammatical blunders in music.)

37. "No devil can compel me to write only cadences of such a kind."

(From notes written in his years of study. Beethoven called the composition of fugues "the art of making musical skeletons.")

38. "Good singing was my guide; I strove to write as flowingly as possible and trusted in my ability to justify myself before the judgment-seat of sound reason and pure taste."

(From notes in the instruction book of Archduke Rudolph.)

39. "Does he believe that I think of a wretched fiddle when the spirit speaks to me?"

(To his friend, the admirable violinist Schuppanzigh, when the latter complained of the difficulty of a passage in one of his works.)

[Beethoven here addresses his friend in the third person, which is the customary style of address for the German nobility and others towards inferiors in rank. H. E. K.]

40. "The Scotch songs show how unconstrainedly irregular melodies can be treated with the help of harmony."

(Diary, 1812–1818. Since 1809 Beethoven had arranged Folksongs for Thomson of Edinburgh.)

41. "To write true church music, look through the old monkish chorals, etc., also the most correct translations of the periods, and perfect prosody in the Catholic Psalms and hymns generally."

(Diary, 1818.)

42. "Many assert that every minor piece must end in the minor. Nego! On the contrary I find that in the soft scales the major third at the close has a glorious and uncommonly quieting effect. Joy follows sorrow, sunshine—rain. It affects me as if I were looking up to the silvery glistering of the evening star."

(From Archduke Rudolph's book of instruction.)

43. "Rigorists, and devotees of antiquity, relegate the perfect fourth to the list of dissonances. Tastes differ. To my ear it gives not the least offence combined with other tones."

(From Archduke Rudolph's book of instruction, compiled in 1809.)

44. "When the gentlemen can think of nothing new, and can go no further, they quickly call in a diminished seventh chord to help them out of the predicament."

(A remark made to Schindler.)

45. "My dear boy, the startling effects which many credit to the natural genius of the composer, are often achieved with the greatest ease by the use and resolution of the diminished seventh chords."

(Reported by Karl Friederich Hirsch, a pupil of Beethoven in the winter of 1816. He was a grandson of Albrechtsberger who had given lessons to Beethoven.)

46. "In order to become a capable composer one must have already learned harmony and counterpoint at the age of from seven to eleven years, so that when the fancy and emotions awake one shall know what to do according to the rules."

(Reported by Schindler as having been put into the mouth of Beethoven by a newspaper of Vienna. Schindler says: "When Beethoven came to Vienna he knew no counterpoint, and little harmony.")

47. "So far as mistakes are concerned it was never necessary for me to learn thorough-bass; my feelings were so sensitive from childhood that I practiced counterpoint without knowing that it must be so or could be otherwise."

(Note on a sheet containing directions for the use of fourths in suspensions—probably intended for the instruction of Archduke Rudolph.)

48. "Continue, Your Royal Highness, to write down briefly your occasional ideas while at the pianoforte. For this a little table alongside the pianoforte is necessary. By this means not only is the fancy strengthened, but one learns to hold fast in a moment the most remote conceptions. It is also necessary to compose without the pianoforte; say often a simple chord melody, with simple harmonies, then figurate according to the rules of counterpoint, and beyond them; this

will give Y. R. H. no headache, but, on the contrary, feeling yourself thus in the midst of art, a great pleasure."

(July 1, 1823, to his pupil Archduke Rudolph.)

49. "The bad habit, which has clung to me from childhood, of always writing down a musical thought which occurs to me, good or bad, has often been harmful to me."

(July 23, 1815, to Archduke Rudolph, while excusing himself for not having visited H.R.H., on the ground that he had been occupied in noting a musical idea which had occurred to him.)

50. "As is my habit, the pianoforte part of the concerto (op. 19) was not written out in the score; I have just written it, wherefore, in order to expedite matters, you receive it in my not too legible handwriting."

(April 22, 1801, to the publisher Hofmeister, in Leipzig.)

51. "Correspondence, as you know, was never my forte; some of my best friends have not had a letter from me in years. I live only in my notes (compositions), and one is scarcely finished when another is begun. As I am working now I often compose three, even four, pieces simultaneously."

(Vienna, June 29, 1800, to Wegeler, in Bonn.)

52. "I never write a work continuously, without interruption. I am always working on several at the same time, taking up one, then another."

(June 1, 1816, to Medical Inspector Dr. Karl von Bursy, when the latter asked about an opera [the book by Berge, sent to Beethoven by Amenda], which was never written.)

53. "I must accustom myself to think out at once the whole, as soon as it shows itself, with all the voices, in my head."

(Note in a sketch-book of 1810, containing studies for the music to "Egmont" and the great Trio in B-flat, op. 97. H. E. K.)

54. "I carry my thoughts about me for a long time, often a very long time, before I write them down; meanwhile my memory is so faithful that I am sure never to forget, not even in years, a theme that has once occurred to me. I change many things, discard, and try again until I am satisfied. Then, however, there begins in my head the development in every direction, and, in as much as I know exactly what I want, the fundamental idea never deserts me,—it arises before me, grows,—I see and hear the picture in all its extent and dimensions stand before my mind like a cast, and there remains for me nothing but the labor of writing it down, which is quickly accomplished when I have the time, for I sometimes take up other work, but never to the confusion of one with the other.

You will ask me where I get my ideas. That I cannot tell you with certainty; they come unsummoned, directly, indirectly,—I could seize

them with my hands,—out in the open air; in the woods; while walk-
ing; in the silence of the nights; early in the morning; incited by moods,
which are translated by the poet into words, by me into tones that
sound, and roar and storm about me until I have set them down in
notes."

(Said to Louis Schlosser, a young musician, whom Beethoven hon-
ored with his friendship in 1822–23.)

55. "On the whole, the carrying out of several voices in strict relationship mutually hinders their progress."

(Fall of 1812, in the Diary of 1812–18.)

56. "Few as are the claims which I make upon such things I shall
still accept the dedication of your beautiful work with pleasure. You
ask, however, that I also play the part of a critic, without thinking that
I must myself submit to criticism! With Voltaire I believe that 'a few
fly-bites can not stop a spirited horse.' In this respect I beg of you to
follow my example. In order not to approach you surreptitiously, but
openly as always, I say that in future works of the character you might
give more heed to the individualization of the voices."

(Vienna, May 10, 1826. To whom the letter was sent is not known,
though from the manner of address it is plain that he was of the
nobility.)

57. "Your variations show talent, but I must fault you for having
changed the theme. Why? What man loves must not be taken away
from him;—moreover to do this is to make changes before variations."

(Baden, July 6, 1804, to Wiedebein, a teacher of music in Brunswick.)

58. "I am not in the habit of rewriting my compositions. I never
did it because I am profoundly convinced that every change of detail
changes the character of the whole."

(February 19, 1813, to George Thomson, who had requested some
changes in compositions submitted to him for publication.)

59. "One must not hold one's self so divine as to be unwilling occasionally to make improvements in one's creations."

(March 4, 1809, to Breitkopf and Hartel, when indicating a few
changes which he wished to have made in the symphonies op. 67
and op. 68.)

60. "The unnatural rage for transcribing pianoforte pieces for string
instruments (instruments that are in every respect so different from
each other) ought to end. I stoutly maintain that only Mozart could
have transcribed his own works, and Haydn; and without putting myself on a level with these great men I assert the same thing about
my pianoforte sonatas. Not only must entire passages be elided and
changed, but additions must be made; and right here lies the rock

of offence to overcome which one must be the master of himself or be possessed of the same skill and inventiveness. I transcribed but a single sonata for string quartet, and I am sure that no one will easily do it after me."

(July 13, 1809, in an announcement of several compositions, among them the quintet op. 29.)

61. "Were it not that my income brings in nothing, I should compose nothing but grand symphonies, church music, or, at the outside, quartets in addition."

(December 20, 1822, to Peters, publisher, in Leipzig. His income had been reduced from 4,000 to 800 florins by the depreciation of Austrian currency.)

[Here, in the original, is one of the puns which Beethoven was fond of making: "Ware mein Gehalt nicht ganzlich ohne Gehalt." H. E. K.])

Chapter 5

On Performing

While reading Beethoven's views on the subject of how music ought to be performed, it is but natural to inquire about his own manner of playing. On this point Ries, his best pupil, reports:

"In general Beethoven played his own compositions very capriciously, yet he adhered, on the whole, strictly to the beat and only at times, but seldom, accelerated the tempo a trifle. Occasionally he would retard the tempo in a crescendo, which produced a very beautiful and striking effect. While playing he would give a passage, now in the right hand, now in the left, a beautiful expression which was simply inimitable; but it was rarely indeed that he added a note or an ornament."

Of his playing when still a young man one of his hearers said that it was in the slow movements particularly that it charmed everybody. Almost unanimously his contemporaries give him the palm for his improvisations. Ries says:

"His extemporizations were the most extraordinary things that one could hear. No artist that I ever heard came at all near the height which Beethoven attained. The wealth of ideas which forced themselves on him, the caprices to which he surrendered himself, the variety of treatment, the difficulties, were inexhaustible."

His playing was not technically perfect. He let many a note "fall under the table," but without marring the effect of his playing. Concerning this we have a remark of his own in No. 75. Somewhat critical is Czerny's report:

"Extraordinary as his extempore playing was it was less successful in the performance of printed compositions; for, since he never took the time or had the patience to practice anything, his success depended mostly on chance and mood; and since, also, his manner of playing as well as composing was ahead of his time, the weak and imperfect pianofortes of his time could not withstand his gigantic style.

It was because of this that Hummel's purling and brilliant manner of play, well adapted to the period, was more intelligible and attractive to the great public. But Beethoven's playing in adagios and legato, in the sustained style, made an almost magical impression on every hearer, and, so far as I know, it has never been surpassed." Czerny's remark about the pianofortes of Beethoven's day explains Beethoven's judgment on his own pianoforte sonatas. He composed for the sonorous pianoforte of the future,—the pianoforte building today.

The following anecdote, told by Czerny, will be read with pleasure. Pleyel, a famous musician, came to Vienna from Paris in 1805, and had his latest quartets performed in the palace of Prince Lobkowitz. Beethoven was present and was asked to play something. "As usual, he submitted to the interminable entreaties and finally was dragged almost by force to the pianoforte by the ladies. Angrily he tears the second violin part of one of the Pleyel quartets from the music-stand where it still lay open, throws it upon the rack of the pianoforte, and begins to improvise. We had never heard him extemporize more brilliantly, with more originality or more grandly than on that evening.

But throughout the entire improvisation there ran in the middle voices, like a thread, or cantus firmus, the insignificant notes, wholly insignificant in themselves, which he found on the page of the quartet, which by chance lay open on the music-stand; on them he built up the most daring melodies and harmonies, in the most brilliant concert style. Old Pleyel could only give expression to his amazement by kissing his hands. After such improvisations Beethoven was wont to break out into a loud and satisfied laugh."

Czerny says further of his playing: "In rapidity of scale passages, trills, leaps, etc., no one equaled him,—not even Hummel. His attitude at the pianoforte was perfectly quiet and dignified, with no approach to grimace, except to bend down a little towards the keys as his deafness increased; his fingers were very powerful, not long, and broadened at the tips by much playing; for he told me often that in his youth he had practiced stupendously, mostly till past midnight. In teaching he laid great stress on a correct position of the fingers (according to the Emanuel Bach method, in which he instructed me); he himself could barely span a tenth. He made frequent use of the pedal, much more frequently than is indicated in his compositions. His reading of the scores of Handel and Gluck and the fugues of Bach was unique, inasmuch as he put a polyphony and spirit into the former which gave the works a new form."

In his later years the deaf master could no longer hear his own playing which therefore came to have a pitifully painful effect. Concerning his manner of conducting, Seyfried says: "It would no wise do to make our master a model in conducting, and the orchestra had to take great care lest it be led astray by its mentor; for he had an eye only for his composition and strove unceasingly by means of manifold gesticulations to bring out the expression which he desired. Often when he reached a forte he gave a violent down beat even if the note were an unaccented one. He was in the habit of marking a diminuendo by crouching down lower and lower, and at a pianissimo he almost crept under the stand. With a crescendo he, too, grew, rising as if out of a stage trap, and with the entrance of a fortissimo he stood on his toes and seemed to take on gigantic proportions, while he waved his arms about as if trying to soar upwards to the clouds. Everything about him was in activity; not a part of his organization remained idle, and the whole man seemed like a perpetuum mobile. Concerning expression, the little nuances, the equable division of light and shade, as also an effective tempo rubato, he was extremely exact and gladly discussed them with the individual members of the orchestra without showing vexation or anger."

62. "It has always been known that the greatest pianoforte players were also the greatest composers; but how did they play? Not like the pianists of today who prance up and down the key-board with passages in which they have exercised themselves,—putsch, putsch, putsch;—what does that mean? Nothing. When the true pianoforte virtuosi played it was always something homogeneous, an entity; it could be transcribed and then it appeared as a well thought-out work. That is pianoforte playing; the other is nothing!"

(In conversation with Tomaschek, October, 1814.)

63. "Candidly I am not a friend of Allegri di bravura and such, since they do nothing but promote mechanism."

(Hetzendorf, July 16, 1823, to Ries in London.)

64. "The great pianists have nothing but technique and affectation."

(Fall of 1817, to Marie Pachler-Koschak, a pianist whom Beethoven regarded very highly. "You will play the sonatas in F major and C minor, for me, will you not?")

65. "As a rule, in the case of these gentlemen, all reason and feeling are generally lost in the nimbleness of their fingers."

(Reported by Schindler as a remark of Beethoven's concerning pianoforte virtuosi.)

66. "Habit may depreciate the most brilliant talents."

(In 1812 to his pupil, Archduke Rudolph, whom he warns against too zealous a devotion to music.)

67. "You will have to play a long time yet before you realize that you can not play at all."

(July, 1808. Reported by Rust as having been said to a young man who played for Beethoven.)

68. "One must be something if one wishes to put on appearances."

(August 15, 1812, to Bettina von Arnim.)

69. "These pianoforte players have their coteries whom they often join; there they are praised continually,—and there's an end of art!"

(Conversation with Tomaschek, October, 1814.)

70. "We Germans have too few dramatically trained singers for the part of Leonore. They are too cold and unfeeling; the Italians sing and act with body and soul."

(1824, in Baden, to Freudenberg, an organist from Breslau.)

71. "If he is a master of his instrument I rank an organist amongst the first of virtuosi. I too, played the organ a great deal when I was young, but my nerves would not stand the power of the gigantic instrument."

(To Freudenberg, in Baden.)

72. "I never wrote noisy music. For my instrumental works I need an orchestra of about sixty good musicians. I am convinced that only such a number can bring out the quickly changing graduations in performance."

(Reported by Schindler.)

73. "A Requiem ought to be quiet music,—it needs no trump of doom; memories of the dead require no hubbub."

(Reported by Holz to Fanny von Ponsing, in Baden, summer of 1858. According to the same authority Beethoven valued Cherubini's "Requiem" more highly than any other.)

74. "No metronome at all! He who has sound feeling needs none, and he who has not will get no help from the metronome;—he'll run away with the orchestra anyway."

(Reported by Schindler. It had been found that Beethoven himself had sent different metronomic indications to the publisher and the Philharmonic Society of London.)

75. "In reading rapidly a multitude of misprints may pass unnoticed because you are familiar with the language."

(To Wegeler, who had expressed wonder at Beethoven's rapid primavista playing, when it was impossible to see each individual note.)

76. "The poet writes his monologue or dialogue in a certain, continuous rhythm, but the elocutionist in order to insure an understanding of the sense of the lines, must make pauses and interruptions at places where the poet was not permitted to indicate it by punctuation. The same manner of declamation can be applied to music, and admits of modification only according to the number of performers."

(Reported by Schindler, Beethoven's faithful factotum.)

77. "With respect to his playing with you, when he has acquired the proper mode of fingering and plays in time and plays the notes with tolerable correctness, only then direct his attention to the matter of interpretation; and when he has gotten this far do not stop him for little mistakes, but point them out at the end of the piece. Although I have myself given very little instruction I have always followed this method which quickly makes musicians, and that, after all, is one of the first objects of art."

(To Czerny, who was teaching music to Beethoven's nephew Karl.)

78. "Always place the hands at the key-board so that the fingers can not be raised higher than is necessary; only in this way is it possible to produce a singing tone."

(Reported by Schindler as Beethoven's view on pianoforte instruction. He hated a staccato style of playing and dubbed it "finger dancing" and "throwing the hands in the air.")

[#79 was skipped in the 1905 edition—error?]

Chapter 6

On His Own Works

80. "I haven't a single friend; I must live alone. But well I know that God is nearer to me than to the others of my art; I associate with Him without fear, I have always recognized and understood Him, and I have no fear for my music,—it can meet no evil fate. Those who understand it must become free from all the miseries that the others drag with them."

(To Bettina von Arnim. [Bettina's letter to Goethe, May 28, 1810.])

81. "The variations will prove a little difficult to play, particularly the trills in the coda; but let that not frighten you. It is so disposed that you need play only the trills, omitting the other notes because they are also in the violin part. I would never have written a thing of this kind had I not often noticed here and there in Vienna a man who after I had improvised of an evening would write down some of my peculiarities and make boast of them next day. Foreseeing that these things would soon appear in print I made up my mind to anticipate them. Another purpose which I had was to embarrass the local pianoforte masters. Many of them are my mortal enemies, and I wanted to have my revenge in this way, for I knew in advance that the variations would be put before them, and that they would make exhibitions of themselves."

(Vienna, November 2, 1793, to Eleonore von Breuning, in dedicating to her the variations in F major, "Se vuol ballare." [The pianist whom Beethoven accuses of stealing his thunder was Abbe Gelinek.])

82. "The time in which I wrote my sonatas (the first ones of the second period) was more poetical than the present (1823); such hints were therefore unnecessary. Every one at that time felt in the Largo of the third sonata in D (op. 10) the pictured soulstate of a melancholy being, with all the nuances of light and shade which occur in a delineation of melancholy and its phases, without requiring a key in the shape of a superscription; and everybody then saw in the two sonatas

(op. 14) the picture of a contest between two principles, or a dialogue between two persons, because it was so obvious."

(In answer to Schindler's question why he had not indicated the poetical conceits underlying his sonatas by superscriptions or titles.)

83. "This sonata has a clean face (literally: 'has washed itself'), my dear brother!"

(January, 1801, to Hofmeister, publisher in Leipzig to whom he offers the sonata, op. 22, for 20 ducats.)

84. "They are incessantly talking about the C-sharp minor sonata (op. 27, No. 2); on my word I have written better ones. The F-sharp major sonata (op. 78) is a different thing!"

(A remark to Czerny.)

[The C-sharp minor sonata is that popularly known as the "Moonlight Sonata," a title which is wholly without warrant. Its origin is due to Rellstab, who, in describing the first movement, drew a picture of a small boat in the moonlight on Lake Lucerne. In Vienna a tradition that Beethoven had composed it in an arbor gave rise to the title "Arbor sonata." Titles of this character work much mischief in the amateur mind by giving rise to fantastic conceptions of the contents of the music. H. E. K.]

85. "The thing which my brother can have from me is 1, a Septett per il Violino, Viola, Violoncello, Contrabasso, Clarinetto, Cornto, Fagotto, tutti obligati; for I can not write anything that is not obligato, having come into the world with obligato accompaniment."

(December 15, 1800, to Hofmeister, publisher, in Leipzig.)

86. "I am but little satisfied with my works thus far; from today I shall adopt a new course."

(Reported by Carl Czerny in his autobiography in 1842. Concerning the time at which the remark was made, Czerny says: "It was said about 1803, when B. had composed op. 28 [the pianoforte sonata in D] to his friend Krumpholz [a violinist]. Shortly afterward there appeared the sonatas [now op. 31] in which a partial fulfillment of his resolution may be observed.")

87. "Read Shakespeare's 'Tempest.'"

(An answer to Schindler's question as to what poetical conceit underlay the sonatas in F minor. Beethoven used playfully to call the little son of Breuning, the friend of his youth, A&Z, because he employed him often as a messenger.)

["Schindler relates that when once he asked Beethoven to tell him what the F minor and D minor (op. 31, No. 2) meant, he received for an answer only the enigmatical remark: 'Read Shakespeare's "Tempest."' Many a student and commentator has since read the 'Tempest' in the hope of finding a clew to the emotional contents which Beethoven believed to be in the two works, so singularly associated, only to find himself baffled. It is a fancy, which rests, perhaps, too much on outward things, but still one full of suggestion, that had Beethoven said: 'Hear my C minor symphony,' he would have given a better starting-point to the imagination of those who are seeking to know what the F minor sonata means. Most obviously it means music, but it means music that is an expression of one of those psychological struggles which Beethoven felt called upon more and more to delineate as he was more and more shut out from the companionship of the external world. Such struggles are in the truest sense of the word tempests. The motive, which, according to the story, Beethoven himself said, indicates, in the symphony, the rappings of Fate at the door of human existence, is common to two works which are also related in their spiritual contents. Singularly enough, too, in both cases the struggle which is begun in the first movement and continued in the third, is interrupted by a period of calm, reassuring, soul-fortifying aspiration, which, in the symphony as well as in the sonata, takes the form of a theme with variations."—"How to Listen to Music," page 29. H. E. K.]

88. "Sinfonia Pastorella. He who has ever had a notion of country life can imagine for himself without many superscriptions what the composer is after. Even without a description the whole, which is more sentiment than tone painting, will be recognized."

(A note among the sketches for the "Pastoral" symphony preserved in the Royal Library at Berlin.)

[There are other notes of similar import among the sketches referred to which can profitably be introduced here:

"The hearer should be allowed to discover the situations;"

"Sinfonia caracteristica, or a recollection of country life;"

"Pastoral Symphony: No picture, but something in which the emotions are expressed which are aroused in men by the pleasure of the country (or) in which some feelings of country life are set forth."

When, finally, the work was given to the publisher, Beethoven included in the title an admonitory explanation which should have everlasting validity: "Pastoral Symphony: more expression of feeling than painting." H. E. K.]

89. "My 'Fidelio' was not understood by the public, but I know that it will yet be appreciated; for though I am well aware of the value of my 'Fidelio' I know just as well that the symphony is my real element. When sounds ring in me I always hear the full orchestra; I can ask anything of instrumentalists, but when writing for the voice I must continually ask myself: 'Can that be sung?'

(A remark made in 1823 or 1824 to Griesinger.)

90. "Thus Fate knocks at the portals!"

(Reported by Schindler as Beethoven's explanation of the opening of the symphony in C minor.)

["Hofrath Kueffner told him (Krenn) that he once lived with Beethoven in Heiligenstadt, and that they were in the habit evenings of going down to Nussdorf to eat a fish supper in the Gasthaus 'Zur Rose.' One evening when B. was in a good humor, Kueffner began: 'Tell me frankly which is your favorite among your symphonies?' B. (in good humor) 'Eh! Eh! The Eroica.' K. 'I should have guessed the C minor.' B. 'No; the Eroica.'" From Thayer's notebook. See "Music and Manners in the Classical Period." H.E.K.]

91. "The solo sonatas (op. 109-ll?) are perhaps the best, but also the last, music that I composed for the pianoforte. It is and always will be an unsatisfactory instrument. I shall hereafter follow the example of my grandmaster Handel, and every year write only an oratorio and a concerto for some string or wind instrument, provided I shall have finished my tenth symphony (C minor) and Requiem."

(Reported by Holz. As to the tenth symphony see note to No. 95.)

92. "God knows why it is that my pianoforte music always makes the worst impression on me, especially when it is played badly."

(June 2, 1804. A note among the sketches for the "Leonore" overture.)

93. "Never did my own music produce such an effect upon me; even now when I recall this work it still costs me a tear."

(Reported by Holz. The reference is to the Cavatina from the quartet in B-flat, op. 130, which Beethoven thought the crown of all quartet movements and his favorite composition. When alone and undisturbed he was fond of playing his favorite pianoforte Andante—that from the sonata op. 28.)

94. "I do not write what I most desire to, but that which I need to because of money. But this is not saying that I write only for money. When the present period is past, I hope at last to write that which is the highest thing for me as well as art,—'Faust.'"

(From a conversation-book used in 1823. To Buhler, tutor in the house of a merchant, who was seeking information about an oratorio which Beethoven had been commissioned to write by the Handel and Haydn Society of Boston.)

95. "Ha! 'Faust;' that would be a piece of work! Something might come out of that! But for some time I have been big with three other large works. Much is already sketched out, that is, in my head. I must be rid of them first:—two large symphonies differing from each other,

and each differing from all the others, and an oratorio. And this will take a long time. you see, for a considerable time I have had trouble to get myself to write. I sit and think, and think I've long had the thing, but it will not on the paper. I dread the beginning of these large works. Once into the work, and it goes."

(In the summer of 1822, to Rochlitz, at Baden. The symphonies referred to are the ninth and tenth. They existed only in Beethoven's mind and a few sketches. In it he intended to combine antique and modern views of life.)

["In the text Greek mythology, cantique ecclesiastique; in the Allegro, a Bacchic festival." (Sketchbook of 1818)]

[The oratorio was to have been called "The Victory of the Cross." It was not written. Schindler wrote to Moscheles in London about Beethoven in the last weeks of his life: "He said much about the plan of the tenth symphony. As the work had shaped itself in his imagination it might have become a musical monstrosity, compared with which his other symphonies would have been mere opuscula."]

Chapter 7

On Art and Artists

96. "How eagerly mankind withdraws from the poor artist what it has once given him;—and Zeus, from whom one might ask an invitation to sup on ambrosia, lives no longer."

(In the summer of 1814, to Kauka, an advocate who represented him in the lawsuit against the heirs of Kinsky.)

97. "I love straightforwardness and uprightness, and believe that the artist ought not to be belittled; for, alas! brilliant as fame is externally, it is not always the privilege of the artist to be Jupiter's guest on Olympus all the time. Unfortunately vulgar humanity drags him down only too often and too rudely from the pure upper ether."

(June 5, 1852, to C. F. Peters, music publisher, in Leipzig when treating with him touching a complete edition of his works.)

98. "The true artist has no pride; unhappily he realizes that art has no limitations, he feels darkly how far he is from the goal, and while, perhaps he is admired by others, he grieves that he has not yet reached the point where the better genius shall shine before him like a distant sun."

(Teplitz, July 17, to an admirer ten years old.)

99. "You yourself know what a change is wrought by a few years in the case of an artist who is continually pushing forward. The greater the progress which one makes in art, the less is one satisfied with one's old works."

(Vienna, August 4, 1800, to Mathisson, in the dedication of his setting of "Adelaide." "My most ardent wish will be fulfilled if you are not displeased with the musical composition of your heavenly 'Adelaide.'")

100. "Those composers are exemplars who unite nature and art in their works."

(Baden, in 1824, to Freudenberg, organist from Breslau.)

101. "What will be the judgment a century hence concerning the lauded works of our favorite composers today? Inasmuch as nearly

everything is subject to the changes of time, and, more's the pity, the fashions of time, only that which is good and true, will endure like a rock, and no wanton hand will ever venture to defile it. Then let every man do that which is right, strive with all his might toward the goal which can never be attained, develop to the last breath the gifts with which a gracious Creator has endowed him, and never cease to learn; for 'Life is short, art eternal!'"

(From the notes in the instruction book of Archduke Rudolph.)

102. "Famous artists always labor under an embarrassment;—therefore first works are the best, though they may have sprung out of dark ground."

(Conversation-book of 1840.)

103. "A musician is also a poet; he also can feel himself transported by a pair of eyes into another and more beautiful world where greater souls make sport of him and set him right difficult tasks."

(August 15, 1812, to Bettina von Arnim.)

104. "I told Goethe my opinion as to how applause affects men like us, and that we want our equals to hear us understandingly! Emotion suits women only; music ought to strike fire from the soul of a man."

(August 15, 1810, to Bettina von Arnim.)

105. "Most people are touched by anything good; but they do not partake of the artist's nature; artists are ardent, they do not weep."

(Reported to Goethe by Bettina von Arnim, May 28, 1810.)

106. "L'art unit tout le monde,—how much more the true artist!"

(March 15, 1823, to Cherubini, in Paris.)

107. "Only the artist, or the free scholar, carries his happiness within him."

(Reported by Karl von Bursy as part of a conversation in 1816.)

108. "There ought to be only one large art warehouse in the world, to which the artist could carry his art-works and from which he could carry away whatever he needed. As it is one must be half a trades-man."

(January, 1801, to Hofmeister, in Leipzig.)

Chapter 8

On the Works of Others

The opinion of artist on artists is a dubious quantity. Recall the startling criticisms of Bocklin on his associates in art made public by the memoirs of his friends after his death. Such judgments are often one-sided, not without prejudice, and mostly the expression of impulse. It is a different matter when the artist speaks about the disciples of another art than his own, even if the opinions which Bocklin and Wagner held of each other are not a favorable example. Where Beethoven speaks of other composers we must read with clear and open eyes; but even here there will be much with which we can be in accord, especially his judgment on Rossini, whom he hated so intensely, and whose airy, sense-bewitching art seduced the Viennese from Beethoven. Interesting and also characteristic of the man is the attitude which he adopted towards the poets of his time. In general he estimated his contemporaries as highly as they deserved.

109. "Do not tear the laurel wreaths from the heads of Handel, Haydn and Mozart; they belong to them,—not yet to me."
(Teplitz, July 17, l852, to his ten-year-old admirer, Emilie M., who had given him a portfolio made by herself.)
110. "Pure church music ought to be performed by voices only, except a 'Gloria,' or some similar text. For this reason I prefer Palestrina; but it is folly to imitate him without having his genius and religious views; it would be difficult, if not impossible, too, for the singers of today to sing his long notes in a sustained and pure manner."
(To Freudenberg, in 1824.)
111. "Handel is the unattained master of all masters. Go and learn from him how to achieve vast effects with simple means."
(Reported by Seyfried. On his death-bed, about the middle of February, 1827, he said to young Gerhard von Breuning, on receiving Handel's works: "Handel is the greatest and ablest of all composers; from him I can still learn. Bring me the books!")

112. "Handel is the greatest composer that ever lived. I would uncover my head and kneel on his grave."

(Fall of 1823, to J. A. Stumpff, harp maker of London, who acted very nobly toward Beethoven in his last days. It was he who rejoiced the dying composer by sending him the forty volumes of Handel's works [see 111].)

["Cipriani Potter, to A. W. T., February 27, 1861. Beethoven used to walk across the fields to Vienna very often. B. would stop, look about and express his love for nature. One day Potter asked: 'Who is the greatest living composer, yourself excepted?' Beethoven seemed puzzled for a moment, and then exclaimed: 'Cherubini!' Potter went on: 'And of dead authors?' B.—He had always considered Mozart as such, but since he had been made acquainted with Handel he put him at the head." From A. W. Thayer's notebook, reprinted in "Music and Manners in the Classical Period," page 208. H.E.K.]

113. "Heaven forbid that I should take a journal in which sport is made of the manes of such a revered one."

(Conversation-book of 1825, in reference to a criticism of Handel.)

114. "That you are going to publish Sebastian Bach's works is something which does good to my heart, which beats in love of the great and lofty art of this ancestral father of harmony; I want to see them soon."

(January, 1801, to Hofmeister, in Leipzig.)

115. "Of Emanuel Bach's clavier works I have only a few, yet they must be not only a real delight to every true artist, but also serve him for study purposes; and it is for me a great pleasure to play works that I have never seen, or seldom see, for real art lovers."

(July 26, 1809, to Gottfried Hartel, of Leipzig in ordering all the scores of Haydn, Mozart and the two Bachs.)

116. "See, my dear Hummel, the birthplace of Haydn. I received it as a gift today, and it gives me great pleasure. A mean peasant hut, in which so great a man was born!"

(Remarked on his death-bed to his friend Hummel.)

117. "I have always reckoned myself among the greatest admirers of Mozart, and shall do so till the day of my death."

(February 6, 1886, to Abbe Maximilian Stadler, who had sent him his essay on Mozart's "Requiem.")

118. "Cramer, Cramer! We shall never be able to compose anything like that!"

(To Cramer, after the two had heard Mozart's concerto in C-minor at a concert in the Augarten.)

119. "'Die Zauberflote' will always remain Mozart's greatest work, for in it he for the first time showed himself to be a German musician.

'Don Juan' still has the complete Italian cut; besides our sacred art ought never permit itself to be degraded to the level of a foil for so scandalous a subject."

(A remark reported by Seyfried.)

["Hozalka says that in 1820–21, as near as he can recollect, the wife of a Major Baumgarten took boy boarders in the house then standing where the Musikverein's Saal now is, and that Beethoven's nephew was placed with her. Her sister, Baronin Born, lived with her. One evening Hozalka, then a young man, called there and found only Baronin Born at home. Soon another caller came and stayed to tea. It was Beethoven. Among other topics Mozart came on the tapis, and the Born asked Beethoven (in writing, of course) which of Mozart's operas he thought most of. 'Die Zauberflote' said Beethoven, and, suddenly clasping his hands and throwing up his eyes, exclaimed: 'Oh, Mozart!'" From A. W. Thayer's notebooks, reprinted in "Music and Manners in the Classical Period," page 198. H. E. K.]

120. "Say all conceivable pretty things to Cherubini,—that there is nothing I so ardently desire as that we should soon get another opera from him, and that of all our contemporaries I have the highest regard for him."

(May 6, 1823, to Louis Schlasser, afterward chapel master in Darmstadt, who was about to undertake a journey to Paris. See note to No. 112.)

121. "Among all the composers alive Cherubini is the most worthy of respect. I am in complete agreement, too, with his conception of the 'Requiem,' and if ever I come to write one I shall take note of many things."

(Remark reported by Seyfried. See No. 112.)

122. "Whoever studies Clementi thoroughly has simultaneously also learned Mozart and other authors; inversely, however, this is not the case."

(Reported by Schindler.)

123. "There is much good in Spontini; he understands theatrical effect and martial noises admirably.

Spohr is so rich in dissonances; pleasure in his music is marred by his chromatic melody.

His name ought not to be Bach (brook), but Ocean, because of his infinite and inexhaustible wealth of tonal combinations and harmonies. Bach is the ideal of an organist."

(In Baden, 1824, to Freudenberg.)

124. "The little man, otherwise so gentle,—I never would have credited him with such a thing. Now Weber must write operas in earnest,

one after the other, without caring too much for refinement! Kaspar, the monster, looms up like a house; wherever the devil sticks in his claw we feel it."

(To Rochlitz, at Baden, in the summer of 1823.)

125. "There you are, you rascal; you're a devil of a fellow, God bless you! . . . Weber, you always were a fine fellow."

(Beethoven's hearty greeting to Karl Maria von Weber, in October, 1823.)

126. "K. M. Weber began too learn too late; art did not have a chance to develop naturally in him, and his single and obvious striving is to appear brilliant."

(A remark reported by Seyfried.)

127. "'Euryanthe' is an accumulation of diminished seventh chords—all little backdoors!"

(Remarked to Schindler about Weber's opera.)

128. "Truly, a divine spark dwells in Schubert!"

(Said to Schindler when the latter made him acquainted with the "Songs of Ossian," "Die Junge Nonne," "Die Burgschaft," of Schubert's "Grenzen der Menschheit," and other songs.)

129. "There is nothing in Meyerbeer; he hasn't the courage to strike at the right time."

(To Tomaschek, in October, 1814, in a conversation about the "Battle of Victoria," at the performance of which, in 1813, Meyerbeer had played the big drum.)

130. "Rossini is a talented and a melodious composer, his music suits the frivolous and sensuous spirit of the times, and his productivity is such that he needs only as many weeks as the Germans do years to write an opera."

(In 1824, at Baden, to Freudenberg.)

131. "This rascal Rossini, who is not respected by a single master of his art!"

(Conversation-book, 1825.)

132. "Rossini would have become a great composer if his teacher had frequently applied some blows ad posteriora."

(Reported by Schindler. Beethoven had been reading the score of "Il Barbiere di Siviglia.")

133. "The Bohemians are born musicians. The Italians ought to take them as models. What have they to show for their famous conservatories? Behold! their idol, Rossini! If Dame Fortune had not given him a pretty talent and amiable melodies by the bushel, what he learned at school would have brought him nothing but potatoes for his big belly."

(In a conversation-book at Haslinger's music shop, where Beethoven frequently visited.)

136. "Goethe has killed Klopstock for me. You wonder? Now you laugh? Ah, because I have read Klopstock. I carried him about with me for years when I walked. What besides? Well, I didn't always understand him. He skips about so; and he always begins so far away, above or below; always Maestoso! D-flat major! Isn't, it so? But he's great, nevertheless, and uplifts the soul. When I couldn't understand him I sort of guessed at him."

(To Rochlitz, in 1822.)

135. "As for me I prefer to set Homer, Klopstock, Schiller, to music; if it is difficult to do, these immortal poets at least deserve it."

(To the directorate of the "Gesellschaft der Musikfreunde" of Vienna, January, 1824, in negotiations for an oratorio, "The Victory of the Cross" [which he had been commissioned to write by the Handel and Haydn Society of Boston. H. E. K.].)

136. "Goethe and Schiller are my favorite poets, as also Ossian and Homer, the latter of whom, unfortunately, I can read only in translation."

(August 8, 1809, to Breitkopf and Hartel.)

137. "Who can sufficiently thank a great poet,—the most valuable jewel of a nation!"

(February 10, 1811, to Bettina von Arnim. The reference was to Goethe.)

138. "When you write to Goethe about me search out all the words which can express my deepest reverence and admiration. I am myself about to write to him about 'Egmont' for which I have composed the music, purely out of love for his poems which make me happy."

(February 10, 1811, to Bettina von Arnim.)

139. "I would have gone to death, yes, ten times to death for Goethe. Then, when I was in the height of my enthusiasm, I thought out my 'Egmont' music. Goethe,—he lives and wants us all to live with him. It is for that reason that he can be composed. Nobody is so easily composed as he. But I do not like to compose songs."

(To Rochlitz, in 1822, when Beethoven recalled Goethe's amiability in Teplitz.)

140. "Goethe is too fond of the atmosphere of the court; fonder than becomes a poet. There is little room for sport over the absurdities of the virtuosi, when poets, who ought to be looked upon as the foremost teachers of the nation, can forget everything else in the enjoyment of court glitter."

(Franzensbrunn, August 9, 1812, to Gottfried Hartel of Leipzig.)

141. "When two persons like Goethe and I meet these grand folk must be made to see what our sort consider great."

(August 15, 1812, in a description of how haughtily he, and how humbly Goethe, had behaved in the presence of the Imperial court.)

142. "Since that summer in Carlsbad I read Goethe every day,—when I read at all."

(Remarked to Rochlitz.)

143. "Goethe ought not to write more; he will meet the fate of the singers. Nevertheless he will remain the foremost poet of Germany."

(Conversationbook, 1818.)

144. "Can you lend me the 'Theory of Colors' for a few weeks? It is an important work. His last things are insipid."

(Conversation-book, 1820.)

145. "After all the fellow writes for money only."

(Reported by Schindler as having been said by Beethoven when, on his death-bed, he angrily threw a book of Walter Scott's aside.)

146. "He, too, then, is nothing better than an ordinary man! Now he will trample on all human rights only to humor his ambition; he will place himself above all others,—become a tyrant!"

(With these words, as testified to by Ries, an eye-witness, Beethoven tore the title-page from the score of his "Eroica" symphony [which bore a dedication to Bonaparte] when the news reached him that Napoleon had declared himself emperor.)

147. "I believe that so long as the Austrian has his brown beer and sausage he will not revolt."

(To Simrock, publisher, in Bonn, August 2, 1794.)

148. "Why do you sell nothing but music? Why did you not long ago follow my well-meant advice? Do get wise, and find your raison. Instead of a hundred-weight of paper order genuine unwatered Regensburger, float this much-liked article of trade down the Danube, serve it in measures, half-measures and seidels at cheap prices, throw in at intervals sausages, rolls, radishes, butter and cheese, invite the hungry and thirsty with letters an ell long on a sign: 'Musical Beer House,' and you will have so many guests at all hours of the day that one will hold the door open for the other and your office will never be empty."

(To Haslinger, the music publisher, when the latter had complained about the indifference of the Viennese to music.)

Chapter 9

On Education

Beethoven's observations on this subject were called out by his experiences in securing an education for his nephew Karl, son of his like-named brother, a duty which devolved on him on the death of his brother in the winter of 1815. He loved his nephew almost to idolatry, and hoped that he would honor the name of Beethoven in the future. But there was a frivolous vein in Karl, inherited probably from his mother, who was on easy footing with morality both before and after her husband's death. She sought with all her might to rid her son of the guardianship of his uncle. Karl was sent to various educational institutions and to these Beethoven sent many letters containing advice and instructions. The nephew grew to be more and more a care, not wholly without fault of the master. His passionate nature led to many quarrels between the two, all of which were followed by periods of extravagant fondness. Karl neglected his studies, led a frivolous life, was fond of billiards and the coffee-houses which were then generally popular, and finally, in the summer of 1826, made an attempt at suicide in the Helenental near Baden, which caused his social ostracism. When he was found he cried out: "I went to the bad because my uncle wanted to better me."

Beethoven succeeded in persuading Baron von Stutterheim, commander of an infantry regiment at Iglau, to accept him as an aspirant for military office. In later life he became a respected official and man. So Beethoven himself was vouchsafed only an ill regulated education. His dissolute father treated him now harshly, now gently. His mother, who died early, was a silent sufferer, had thoroughly understood her son, and to her his love was devotion itself. He labored unwearyingly at his own intellectual and moral advancement until his death.

It seems difficult to reconcile his almost extravagant estimate of the greatest possible liberty in the development of man with his demands for strict constraint to which he frequently gives expression; but he had recognized that it is necessary to grow out of restraint into liberty. His model as a sensitive and sympathetic educator was his motherly friend, the wife of Court Councillor von Breuning in Bonn, of whom he once said: "She knew how to keep the insects off the blossoms."

Beethoven's views on musical education are to be found in the chapters "On Composition" and "On Performing Music."

149. "Like the State, each man must have his own constitution." (Diary, 1815.)

150. "Recommend virtue to your children; that, alone can bring happiness; not wealth,—I speak from experience. It was virtue alone that bore me up in my misery; to her and my art I owe that I did not end my life by self-murder."
(October 6, 1802, to his brothers Karl and Johann [the so-called Heiligenstadt Will].)

151. "I know no more sacred duty than to rear and educate a child." (January 7, 1820, in a communication to the Court of Appeals in the suit touching the guardianship of his nephew Karl.)

152. "Nature's weaknesses are nature's endowments; reason, the guide, must seek to lead and lessen them."
(Diary, 1817.)

153. "It is man's habit to hold his fellow man in esteem because he committed no greater errors."
(May 6, 1811, to Breitkopf and Hartel, in a letter complaining of faulty printing in some of his compositions.)

154. "There is nothing more efficient in enforcing obedience upon others than the belief on their part that you are wiser than they . . . Without tears fathers can not inculcate virtue in their children, or teachers learning and wisdom in their pupils; even the laws, by compelling tears from the citizens, compel them also to strive for justice."
(Diary, 1815.)

155. "It is only becoming in a youth to combine his duties toward education and advancement with those which he owes to his benefactor and supporter; this I did toward my parents."
(May 19, 1825, to his nephew Karl.)

156. "You can not honor the memory of your father better than to continue your studies with the greatest zeal, and strive to become an honest and excellent man."
(To his nephew, 1816–18.)

157. "Let your conduct always be amiable; through art and science the best and noblest of men are bound together and your future vocation will not exclude you."

(Baden, July 18, 1825, to his nephew, who had decided to become a merchant.)

158. "It is very true that a drop will hollow a stone; a thousand lovely impressions are obliterated when children are placed in wooden institutions while they might receive from their parents the most soulful impressions which would continue to exert their influence till the latest age."

(Diary, spring of 1817. Beethoven was dissatisfied with Giannatasio's school in which he had placed his nephew. "Karl is a different child after he has been with me a few hours" [Diary]. In 1826, after the attempt at suicide, Beethoven said to Breuning: "My Karl was in an institute; educational institutions furnish forth only hot house plants.")

159. "Drops of water wear away a stone in time, not by force but by continual falling. Only through tireless industry are the sciences achieved so that one can truthfully say: no day without its line,—nulla dies sine linea."

(1799, in a sketch for a theoretical handbook for Archduke Rudolph.)

Chapter 10

On Beethoven

So open-hearted and straightforward a character as Beethoven could not have pictured himself with less reserve or greater truthfulness than he did during his life. Frankness toward himself, frankness toward others (though sometimes it went to the extreme of rudeness and ill-breeding) was his motto. The joyous nature which was his as a lad, and which was not at all averse to a merry prank now and then, underwent a change when he began to lose his hearing. The dread of deafness and its consequences drove him nearly to despair, so that he sometimes contemplated suicide. Increasing hardness of hearing gradually made him reserved, morose and gloomy. With the progress of the malady his disposition and character underwent a decided change,—a fact which may be said to account for the contradictions in his conduct and utterances. It made him suspicious, distrustful; in his later years he imagined himself cheated and deceived in the most trifling matters by relatives, friends, publishers, servants.

Nevertheless Beethoven's whole soul was filled with a high idealism which penetrated through the miseries of his daily life; it was full, too, of a great love toward humanity in general and his unworthy nephew in particular. Towards his publishers he often appeared covetous and grasping, seeking to rake and scrape together all the money possible; but this was only for the purpose of assuring the future of his nephew. At the same time, in a merry moment, he would load down his table with all that kitchen and cellar could provide, for the reflection of his friends. Thus he oscillated continuously between two extremes; but the power which swung the pendulum was always the aural malady. He grew peevish and capricious towards his best friends, rude, even brutal at times in his treatment of them; only in the next moment to overwhelm them most pathetically with attentions. Till the end of his life he remained a sufferer from his passionate disposition over which he gradually obtained control until, at the end, one could almost speak of a sunny clarification of his nature.

He has heedlessly been accused of having led a dissolute life, of having been an intemperate drinker. There would be no necessity of contradicting such a charge even if there were a scintilla of evidence to support it; a drinker is not necessarily a dishonorable man, least of all a musician who drinks. But, the fact of the matter is that it is not true. If once Beethoven wrote a merry note about merrymaking with friends, let us rejoice that occasions did sometimes occur, though but rarely, when the heart of the sufferer was temporarily gladdened.

He was a strict moralist, as is particularly evidenced by the notes in his journal which have not been made public. In many things which befell him in his daily life he was as ingenuous as a child. His personality, on the whole, presented itself in such a manner as to invite the intellectual and social Philistine to call him a fool.

160. "I shall print a request in all the newspapers that henceforth all artists refrain from painting my picture without my knowledge; I never thought that my own face would bring me embarrassment."

(About 1803, to Christine Gerardi, because without his knowledge a portrait of him had been made somewhere—in a cafe, probably.)

161. "Pity that I do not understand the art of war as well as I do the art of music; I should yet conquer Napoleon!"

(To Krumpholz, the violinist, when he informed Beethoven of the victory of Napoleon at Jena.)

162. "If I were a general and knew as much about strategy as I, a composer, know about counterpoint, I'd give you fellows something to do."

(Called out behind the back of a French officer, his fist doubled, on May 12, 1809, when the French had occupied Vienna. Reported by a witness, W. Rust.)

163. "Camillus, if I am not mistaken, was the name of the Roman who drove the wicked Gauls from Rome. At such a cost I would also take the name if I could drive them wherever I found them to where they belong."

(To Pleyel, publisher, in Paris, April, 1807.)

164. "I love most the realm of mind which, to me, is the highest of all spiritual and temporal monarchies."

(To Advocate Kauka in the summer of 1814. He had been speaking about the monarchs represented in the Congress of Vienna.)

165. "I shall not come in person, since that would be a sort of farewell, and farewells I have always avoided."

(January 24, 1818, to Giannatasio del Rio, on taking his nephew Karl out of the latter institute.)

166. "I hope still to bring a few large works into the world, and then, like an old child, to end my earthly career somewhere among good people."

(October 6, 1802, to Wegeler.)

167. "O ye men, who think or declare me to be hostile, morose or misanthropical, what injustice ye do me. Ye know not the secret cause of what thus appears to you. My heart and mind were from childhood disposed for the tender feelings of benevolence; I was always wishing to accomplish great deeds."

(October 6, 1802, in the so-called Heiligenstadt Will.)

168. "Divinity, thou lookest into my heart, thou knowest it, thou knowest that love for mankind and a desire to do good have their abode there. O ye men, when one day ye read this think that ye have wronged me, and may the unfortunate console himself with the thought that he has found one of his kind who, despite all the obstacles which nature put in his path, yet did all in his power to be accepted in the ranks of worthy artists and men!"

(From the Heiligenstadt Will.)

169. "I spend all my mornings with the muses;—and they bless me also in my walks."

(October 12, 1835, to his nephew Karl.)

170. "Concerning myself nothing,—that is, from nothing nothing."

(October 19, 1815, to Countess Erdody.)

[A possible allusion to the line, "Nothing can come of nothing." from Shakespeare's "King Lear," Act 1, scene 1]

171. "Beethoven can write, thank God; but do nothing else on earth."

(December 22, 1822, to Ferdinand Ries, in London.)

172. "Mentally I often frame an answer, but when I come to write it down I generally throw the pen aside, since I am not able to write what I feel."

(October 7, 1826, to his friend Wegeler, in Coblenz. "The better sort of people, I think, know me anyhow." He is excusing his laziness in letter-writing.)

173. "I have the gift to conceal my sensitiveness touching a multitude of things; but when I am provoked at a moment when I am more sensitive than usual to anger, I burst out more violently than anybody else."

(July 24, 1804, to Ries, in reporting to him a quarrel with Stephan von Breuning.)

174. "X. is completely changed since I threw half a dozen books at her head. Perhaps something of their contents accidentally got into her head or her wicked heart."

(To Mme. Streicher, who often had to put Beethoven's house in order.)

175. "I can have no intercourse, and do not want to have any, with persons who are not willing to believe in me because I have not yet made a wide reputation."

(To Prince Lobkowitz, about 1798. A cavalier had failed to show him proper respect in the Prince's salon.)

176. "Many a vigorous and unconsidered word drops from my mouth, for which reason I am considered mad."

(In the summer of 1880, to Dr. Muller, of Bremen, who was paying him a visit.)

177. "I will grapple with Fate; it shall not quite bear me down. O, it is lovely to live life a thousand times!"

(November 16, 1800, or 1801, to Wegeler.)

178. "Morality is the strength of men who distinguish themselves over others, and it is mine."

(In a communication to his friend, Baron Zmeskall.)

179. "I, too, am a king!"

(Said to Holz, when the latter begged him not to sell the ring which King Frederick William III, of Prussia, had sent to him instead of money or an order in return for the dedication of the ninth symphony. "Master, keep the ring," Holz had said, "it is from a king." Beethoven made his remark "with indescribable dignity and self-consciousness.")

[On his deathbed he said to little Gerhard von Breuning: "Know that I am an artist."]

[At the height of the popular infatuation for Rossini (1822) he said to his friends: "Well, they will not be able to rob me of my place in the history of art."]

180. "Prince, what you are you are by accident of birth; what I am, I am through my own efforts. There have been thousands of princes and will be thousands more; there is only one Beethoven!"

(According to tradition, from a letter which he wrote to Prince Lichnowsky when the latter attempted to persuade him to play for some French officers on his estate in Silesia. Beethoven went at night to Troppau, carrying the manuscript of the [so-called] "Appassionata" sonata, which suffered from the rain.)

181. "My nobility is here, and here (pointing to his heart and head)."

(Reported by Schindler. In the lawsuit against his sister-in-law [the mother of nephew Karl] Beethoven had been called on to prove that the "van" in his name was a badge of nobility.)

182. "You write that somebody has said that I am the natural son of the late King of Prussia. The same thing was said to me long ago, but

I have made it a rule never to write anything about myself or answer anything that is said about me."

(October 7, 1826, to Wegeler.)

["I leave it to you to give the world an account of myself and especially my mother." The statement had appeared in Brockhaus's "Lexicon."]

183. "To me the highest thing, after God, is my honor."

(July 26, 1822, to the publisher Peters, in Leipzig.)

184. "I have never thought of writing for reputation and honor. What I have in my heart must out; that is the reason why I compose."

(Remark to Karl Czerny, reported in his autobiography.)

185. "I do not desire that you shall esteem me greater as an artist, but better and more perfect as a man; when the condition of our country is somewhat better, then my art shall be devoted to the welfare of the poor."

(Vienna, June 29, 1800, to Wegeler, in Bonn, writing of his return to his native land.)

186. "Perhaps the only thing that looks like genius about me is that my affairs are not always in the best of order, and that in this respect nobody can be of help but myself."

(April 22, 1801, to Hofmeister, in Leipzig excusing himself for dilatoriness in sending him these compositions: the Pianoforte sonata op. 22, the symphony op. 21, the septet op. 20 and the concerto op. 19.)

187. "I am free from all small vanities. Only in the divine art is the lever which gives me power to sacrifice the best part of my life to the celestial muses."

(September 9, 1824, to George Nigeli, in Zurich.)

188. "Inasmuch as the purpose of the undersigned throughout his career has not been selfish but the promotion of the interests of art, the elevation of popular taste and the flight of his own genius toward loftier ideals and perfection, it was inevitable that he should frequently sacrifice his own advantages and profit to the muse."

(December, 1804, to the Director of the Court Theatre, applying for an engagement which was never effected.)

189. "From my earliest childhood my zeal to serve suffering humanity with my art was never content with any kind of a subterfuge; and no other reward is needed than the internal satisfaction which always accompanies such a deed."

(To Procurator Varenna, who had asked him for compositions to be played at a charity concert in Graz.)

190. "There is no greater pleasure for me than to practice and exhibit my art."

(November 16, 1800, or 1801, to Wegeler.)

191. "I recognize no other accomplishments or advantages than those which place one amongst the better class of men; where I find them, there is my home."

(Teplitz, July 17, 1812, to his little admirer, Emile M., in H.)

192. "From childhood I learned to love virtue, and everything beautiful and good."

(About 1808, to Frau Marie Bigot.)

193. "It is one of my foremost principles never to occupy any other relations than those of friendship with the wife of another man. I should never want to fill my heart with distrust towards those who may chance some day to share my fate with me, and thus destroy the loveliest and purest life for myself."

(About 1808, to Frau Marie Bigot, after she had declined his invitation to drive with him.)

194. "In my solitude here I miss my roommate, at least at evening and noon, when the human animal is obliged to assimilate that which is necessary to the production of the intellectual, and which I prefer to do in company with another."

(Teplitz, September 6, 1811, to Tiedge.)

195. "It was not intentional and premeditated malice which led me to act toward you as I did; it was my unpardonable carelessness."

(To Wegeler.)

196. "I am not bad; hot blood is my wickedness, my crime is youthfulness. I am not bad, really not bad; even though wild surges often accuse my heart, it still is good. To do good wherever we can, to love liberty above all things, and never to deny truth though it be at the throne itself.—Think occasionally of the friend who honors you."

(Written in the autograph album of a Herr Bocke.)

197. "It is a singular sensation to see and hear one's self praised, and then to be conscious of one's own imperfections as I am. I always regard such occasions as admonitions to get nearer the unattainable goal set for us by art and nature, hard as it may be."

(To Mdlle. de Girardi, who had sung his praises in a poem.)

198. "It is my sincere desire that whatever shall be said of me hereafter shall adhere strictly to the truth in every respect regardless of who may be hurt thereby, me not excepted."

(Reported by Schindler, who also relates that when Beethoven handed him documents to be used in the biography a week before his death, he said to him and Breuning: "But in all things severely the truth; for that I hold you to a strict accountability.")

199. "Now you can help me to find a wife. If you find a beautiful woman in F. who, mayhap, endows my music with a sigh,—but she

must be no Elise Burger—make a provisional engagement. But she must be beautiful, for I can love only the beautiful; otherwise I might love myself."

(In 1809, to Baron von Gleichenstein. As for the personal reference it seems likely that Beethoven referred to Elise Burger, second wife of the poet G. August Burger, with whom he had got acquainted after she had been divorced and become an elocutionist.)

200. "Am I not a true friend? Why do you conceal your necessities from me? No friend of mine must suffer so long as I have anything."

(To Ferdinand Ries, in 1801. Ries's father had been kind to Beethoven on the death of his mother in 1787.)

201. "I would rather forget what I owe to myself than what I owe to others."

(To Frau Streicher, in the summer of 1817.)

202. "I never practice revenge. When I must antagonize others I do no more than is necessary to protect myself against them, or prevent them from doing further evil."

(To Frau Streicher, in reference to the troubles which his servants gave him, many of which, no doubt, were due to faults of his own, excusable in a man in his condition of health.)

203. "Be convinced that mankind, even in your case, will always be sacred to me."

(To Czapka, Magisterial Councillor, August, 1826, in the matter of his nephew's attempt at suicide.)

204. "H. is, and always will be, too weak for friendship, and I look upon him and Y. as mere instruments upon which I play when I feel like it; but they can never be witnesses of my internal and external activities, and just as little real participants. I value them according as they do me service."

(Summer of 1800, to the friend of his youth, Pastor Amenda. H. was probably the faithful Baron Zmeskall von Domanovecz.)

205. "If it amuses them to talk and write about me in that manner, let them go on."

(Reported by Schindler as referring to critics who had declared him ripe for the madhouse.)

206. "To your gentlemen critics I recommend a little more foresight and shrewdness, particularly in respect of the products of younger authors, as many a one, who might otherwise make progress, may be frightened off. So far as I am concerned I am far from thinking myself so perfect as not to be able to endure faulting; yet at the beginning the clamor of your critic was so debasing that I could scarcely discuss the matter when I compared myself with others, but had to remain quiet

and think: they do not understand. I was the more able to remain quiet when I recalled how men were praised who signify little among those who know, and who have almost disappeared despite their good points. Well, pax vobiscum, peace to them and me,—I would never have mentioned a syllable had you not begun."

(April 22, 1801, to Breitkopf and Hartel, publishers of the "Allgemeine Musik Zeitung.")

207. "Who was happier than I when I could still pronounce the sweet word 'mother' and have it heard? To whom can I speak it now?"

(September 15, 1787, from Bonn to Dr. Schade, of Augsburg, who had aided him in his return journey from Vienna to Bonn. His mother had died on July 17, 1787.)

208. "I seldom go anywhere since it was always impossible for me to associate with people where there was not a certain exchange of ideas."

(February 15, 1817, to Brentano of Frankfurt.)

209. "Not a word about rest! I know of none except in sleep, and sorry enough am I that I am obliged to yield up more to it than formerly."

(November 16, 1801, or 1802, to Wegeler. In Homer's "Odyssey" Beethoven thickly underscored the words: "Too much sleep is injurious." XV, 393.)

210. "Rest assured that you are dealing with a true artist who likes to be paid decently, it is true, but who loves his own reputation and also the fame of his art; who is never satisfied with himself and who strives continually to make even greater progress in his art."

(November 23, 1809, to George Thomson, of Edinburgh, for whom Beethoven arranged the Scotch songs.)

211. "My motto is always: nulla die sine linea; and if I permit the muse to go to sleep it is only that she may awake strengthened."

(October 7, 1826, to Wegeler.)

212. "There is no treatise likely to be too learned for me. Without laying claim to real learning it is yet true that since my childhood I have striven to learn the minds of the best and wisest of every period of time. It is a disgrace for every artist who does not try to do as much."

(November 2, 1809, to Breitkopf and Hartel, of Leipzig.)

213. "Without wishing in the least to set myself up as an exemplar I assure you that I lived in a small and insignificant place, and made out of myself nearly all that I was there and am here;—this to your comfort in case you feel the need of making progress in art."

(Baden, July 6, 1804, to Herr Wiedebein, of Brunswick, who had asked if it was advisable for a music teacher and student to make his home in Vienna.)

214. "There is much on earth to be done,—do it soon! I must not continue my present everyday life,—art asks this sacrifice also. Take rest in diversion in order to work more energetically."

(Diary, 1814.)

215. "The daily grind exhausts me."

(Baden, August 23, 1823, to his nephew Karl.)

Chapter 11

On Suffering

216. "Compelled to be a philosopher as early as my 28th year;—it is not an easy matter,—more difficult for the artist than any other man."
   (October 6, 1802; the Heiligenstadt Will.)
   217. "Compelled to contemplate a lasting malady, born with an ardent and lively temperament, susceptible to the diversions of society, I was obliged at an early date to isolate myself and live a life of solitude."
(From the same.)
   218. "It was impossible for me to say to others: speak louder; shout! for I am deaf. Ah! was it possible for me to proclaim a deficiency in that one sense which in my case ought to have been more perfect than in all others, which I had once possessed in greatest perfection, to a degree of perfection, indeed, which few of my profession have ever enjoyed?"
(From the same.)
   219. "For me there can be no recreation in human society, refined conversation, mutual exchange of thoughts and feelings; only so far as necessity compels may I give myself to society,—I must live like an exile."
(From the same.)
   220. "How great was the humiliation when one who stood beside me heard the distant sound of a shepherd's pipe, and I heard nothing; or heard the shepherd singing, and I heard nothing. Such experiences brought me to the verge of despair;—but little more and I should have put an end to my life. Art, art alone deterred me."
(From the same.)
   221. "I may say that I live a wretched existence. For almost two years I have avoided all social gatherings because it is impossible for me to tell the people I am deaf. If my vocation were anything else it might be more endurable, but under the circumstances the condition is terrible;

besides what would my enemies say,—they are not few in number! To give you an idea of this singular deafness let me tell you that in the theatre I must lean over close to the orchestra in order to understand the actor; if I am a little remote from them I do not hear the high tones of instruments and voices; it is remarkable that there are persons who have not observed it, but because I am generally absent-minded my conduct is ascribed to that."

(Vienna, June 29, 1800, to Wegeler. "To you only do I confide this as a secret." Concerning his deafness see Appendix.)

222. "My defective hearing appeared everywhere before me like a ghost; I fled from the presence of men, was obliged to appear to be a misanthrope although I am so little such."

(November 16, 1801, or 1800, to Wegeler, in writing to him about his happy love. "Unfortunately, she is not of my station in life.")

223. "Truly, a hard lot has befallen me! Yet I accept the decree of Fate, and continually pray to God to grant that as long as I must endure this death in life, I may be preserved from want."

(March 14, 1827, to Moscheles, after Beethoven had undergone the fourth operation for dropsy and was confronting the fifth. He died on March 26, 1827.)

224. "Live alone in your art! Restricted though you be by your defective sense, this is still the only existence for you."

(Diary, 1816.)

225. "Dissatisfied with many things, more susceptible than any other person and tormented by my deafness, I often find only suffering in the association with others."

(In 1815, to Brauchle, tutor in the house of Countess Erdody.)

226. "I have emptied a cup of bitter suffering and already won martyrdom in art through the kindness of art's disciples and my art associates."

(In the summer of 1814, to Advocate Kauka. "Socrates and Jesus were my exemplars," he remarks in a conversation-book of 1819.)

227. "Perfect the ear trumpets as far as possible, and then travel; this you owe to yourself, to mankind and to the Almighty! Only thus can you develop all that is still locked within you;—and a little court,—a little chapel,—writing the music and having it performed to the glory of the Almighty, the Eternal, the Infinite—"

(Diary, 1815. Beethoven was hoping to receive an appointment as chapelmaster from his former pupil, Archduke Rudolph, Archbishop of Olmutz.)

228. "God help me. Thou seest me deserted by all mankind. I do not want to do wrong,—hear my prayer to be with my Karl in the

future for which there seems to be no possibility now. O, harsh Fate, cruel destiny. No, my unhappy condition will never end. 'This I feel and recognize clearly: Life is not the greatest of blessings; but the greatest of evils is guilt.' (From Schiller's "Braut von Messina"). There is no salvation for you except to hasten away from here; only by this means can you lift yourself again to the heights of your art whereas you are here sinking to the commonplace,—and a symphony—and then away,—away,—meanwhile fund the salaries which can be done for years. Work during the summer preparatory to travel; only thus can you do the great work for your poor nephew; later travel through Italy, Sicily, with a few other artists."

(Diary, spring of 1817. The salaries were the annuities paid him for several years by Archduke Rudolph, Prince Rinsky and Prince Lobkowitz. Seume's "Spaziergang nach Syrakus" was a favorite book of Beethoven's and inspired him in a desire to make a similar tour, but nothing came of it.)

229. "You must not be a man like other men: not for yourself, only for others; for you there is no more happiness except in yourself, in your art.—O God, give me strength to overcome myself, nothing must hold me to this life."

(Beginning of the Diary, 1812–18.)

230. "Leave operas and all else alone, write only for your orphan, and then a cowl to close this unhappy life."

(Diary, 1816.)

231. "I have often cursed my existence; Plutarch taught me resignation. I shall, if possible, defy Fate, though there will be hours in my life when I shall be the most miserable of God's creatures. Resignation! What a wretched resort; yet it is the only one left me!"

(Vienna, June 29, 1800, to Wegeler.)

232. "Patience, they tell me, I must now choose for a guide. I have done so. It shall be my resolve, lastingly, I hope, to endure until it pleases the implacable Parca: to break the thread. There may be improvement,—perhaps not,—I am prepared."

(From the Heiligenstadt Will.)

233. "Let all that is called life be offered to the sublime and become a sanctuary of art. Let me live, even through artificial means, so they can be found."

(Diary, 1814, when Beethoven was being celebrated extraordinarily by the royalties and dignitaries gathered at the Congress of Vienna.)

234. "Ah! it seemed impossible for me to leave the world until I had produced all that I felt called upon to produce; and so I prolonged this wretched existence."

(From the Heiligenstadt Will.)

235. "With joy shall I hasten forward to meet death; if he comes before I shall have had an opportunity to develop all my artistic capabilities, he will come too early in spite of my harsh fate, and I shall probably wish him to come at a later date. But even then I shall be content, for will he not release me from endless suffering? Come when you please, I shall meet you bravely."

(From the Heiligenstadt Will.)

236. "Apollo and the muses will not yet permit me to be delivered over to the grim skeleton, for I owe them so much, and I must, on any departure for the Elysian Fields, leave behind me all that the spirit has inspired and commanded to be finished."

(September 17, 1824, to Schott, music publisher in Mayence.)

237. "Had I not read somewhere that it is not pending man to part voluntarily from his life so long as there is a good deed which he can perform, I should long since have been no more, and by my own hand. O, how beautiful life is, but in my case it is poisoned."

(May 2, 1810, to his friend Wegeler, to whom he is lamenting over "the demon that has set up his habitat in my ears.")

238. "I must abandon wholly the fond hope, which I brought hither, to be cured at least in a degree. As the fallen autumn leaves have withered, so arc now my hopes blighted. I depart in almost the same condition in which I came; even the lofty courage which often animated me in the beautiful days of summer has disappeared."

(From the Will. Beethoven had tried the cure at Heiligenstadt.)

239. "All week long I had to suffer and endure like a saint. Away with this rabble! What a reproach to our civilization that we need what we despise and must always know it near!"

(In 1825, complaining of the misery caused by his domestics.)

240. "The best thing to do not to think of your malady is to keep occupied."

(Diary, 1812–18.)

241. "It is no comfort for men of the better sort to say to them that others also suffer; but, alas! comparisons must always be made, though they only teach that we all suffer, that is err, only in different ways."

(In 1816, to Countess Erdody, on the death of her son.)

242. "The portraits of Handel, Bach, Gluck, Mozart and Haydn in my room,—they may help me to make claim on toleration."

(Diary, 1815–16.)

243. "God, who knows my innermost soul, and knows how sacredly I have fulfilled all the duties but upon me as man by humanity, God and nature will surely some day relieve me from these afflictions."

(July 18, 1821, to Archduke Rudolph, from Unterubling.)

244. "Friendship and similar sentiments bring only wounds to me. Well, so be it; for you, poor Beethoven, there is no outward happiness; you must create it within you,—only in the world of ideality shall you find friends."

(About 1808, to Baron von Gleichenstein, by whom he thought himself slighted.)

245. "You are living on a quiet sea, or already in the safe harbor; you do not feel the distress of a friend out in the raging storm,—or you must not feel it."

(In 1811, to his friend Gleichenstein, when Beethoven was in love with the Baron's sister-in-law, Therese Malfatti.)

246. "I must have a confidant at my side lest life become a burden."

(July 4, 1812, to Count Brunswick, whom he is urging to make a tour with him, probably to Teplitz.)

247. "Your love makes me at once the happiest and the unhappiest of men. At my age I need a certain uniformity and equableness of life; can such exist in our relationship?"

[June 7, 1800?], to the "Immortal Beloved.")

248. "O Providence! vouchsafe me one day of pure joy! Long has the echo of perfect felicity been absent from my heart. When O, when, O Thou Divine One, shall I feel it again in nature's temple and man's? Never? Ah! that would be too hard!"

(Conclusion of the Heiligenstadt Will.)

Chapter 12

On Wisdom

249. "Freedom,—progress, is purpose in the art-world as in universal creation, and if we moderns have not the hardihood of our ancestors, refinement of manners has surely accomplished something."

(Middling, July 29, 1819, to Archduke Rudolph.)

250. "The boundaries are not yet fixed which shall call out to talent and industry: thus far and no further!"

(Reported by Schindler.)

251. "You know that the sensitive spirit must not be bound to miserable necessities."

(In the summer of 1814, to Johann Kauka, the advocate who represented him in the prosecution of his claims against the heirs of Prince Kinsky.)

252. "Art, the persecuted one, always finds an asylum. Did not Daedalus, shut up in the labyrinth, invent the wings which carried him out into the open air? O, I shall find them, too, these wings!"

(February 19, 1812, to Zmeskall, when, in 1811, by decree of the Treasury, the value of the Austrian currency was depreciated one-fifth, and the annuity which Beethoven received from Archduke Rudolph and the Princes Lobkowitz and Kinsky reduced to 800 florins.)

253. "Show me the course where at the goal there stands the palm of victory! Lend sublimity to my loftiest thoughts, bring to them truths that shall live forever!"

(Diary, 1814, while working on "Fidelio.")

254. "Every day is lost in which we do not learn something useful. Man has no nobler or more valuable possession than time; therefore never put off till tomorrow what you can do today."

(From the notes in Archduke Rudolph's instruction book.)

255. "This is the mark of distinction of a truly admirable man: steadfastness in times of trouble."

(Diary, 1816.)

256. "Courage, so it be righteous, will gain all things."
(April, 1815, to Countess Erdody.)

257. "Force, which is a unit, will always prevail against the majority which is divided."
(Conversation-book, 1819.)

258. "Kings and Princes can create professors and councillors, and confer orders and decorations; but they can not create great men, spirits that rise above the earthly rabble; these they can not create, and therefore they are to be respected."
(August 15, 1812, to Bettina von Arnim.)

259. "Man, help yourself!"
(Written under the words: "Fine, with the help of God," which Moscheles had written at the end of a pianoforte arrangement of a portion of "Fidelio.")

260. "If I could give as definite expression to my thoughts about my illness as to my thoughts in music, I would soon help myself."
(September, 1812, to Amalie Sebald, a patient at the cure in Teplitz.)

261. "Follow the advice of others only in the rarest cases."
(Diary, 1816.)

262. "The moral law in us, and the starry sky above us."—Kant.
(Conversation-book, February, 1820.)
[Literally the passage in Kant's "Critique of Practical Reason" reads as follows: "Two things fill the soul with ever new and increasing wonder and reverence the oftener the mind dwells upon them:—the starry sky above me and the moral law in me."]

263. "Blessed is he who has overcome all passions and then proceeds energetically to perform his duties under all circumstances careless of success! Let the motive lie in the deed, not in the outcome. Be not one of those whose spring of action is the hope of reward. Do not let your life pass in inactivity. Be industrious, do your duty, banish all thoughts as to the results, be they good or evil; for such equanimity is attention to intellectual things. Seek an asylum only in Wisdom; for he who is wretched and unhappy is so only in consequence of things. The truly wise man does not concern himself with the good and evil of this world. Therefore endeavor diligently to preserve this use of your reason—for in the affairs of this world, such a use is a precious art."
(Diary. Though essentially in the language of Beethoven there is evidence that the passage was inspired by something that he had read.)

264. "The just man must be able also to suffer injustice without deviating in the least from the right course."
(To the Viennese magistrate in the matter of Karl's education.)

265. "Man's humility towards man pains me; and yet when I consider myself in connection with the universe, what am I and what is

he whom we call the greatest? And yet here, again, lies the divine element in man."

(To the "Immortal Beloved," July 6 [1800?].)

266. "Only the praise of one who has enjoyed praise can give pleasure."

(Conversation-book, 1825.)

267. "Nothing is more intolerable than to be compelled to accuse one's self of one's own errors."

(Teplitz, September 6, 1811, to Tiedge. Beethoven regrets that through his own fault he had not made Tiedge's acquaintance on an earlier opportunity.)

268. "What greater gift can man receive than fame, praise and immortality?"

(Diary, 1816–17. After Pliny, Epist. III.)

269. "Frequently it seems as if I should almost go mad over my undeserved fame; fortune seeks me out and I almost fear new misfortune on that account."

(July, 1810, to his friend Zmeskall. "Every day there come new inquiries from strangers, new acquaintances new relationships.")

270. "The world must give one recognition,—it is not always unjust. I care nothing for it because I have a higher goal."

(August 15, 1812, to Bettina von Arnim.)

271. "I have the more turned my gaze upwards; but for our own sakes and for others we are obliged to turn our attention sometimes to lower things; this, too, is a part of human destiny."

(February 8, 1823, to Zelter, with whom he is negotiating the sale of a copy of the Mass in D.)

272. "Why so many dishes? Man is certainly very little higher than the other animals if his chief delights are those of the table."

(Reported by J. A. Stumpff, in the "Harmonicon" of 1824. He dined with Beethoven in Baden.)

273. "Whoever tells a lie is not pure of heart, and such a person can not cook a clean soup."

(To Mme. Streicher, in 1817, or 1818, after having dismissed an otherwise good housekeeper because she had told a falsehood to spare his feelings.)

274. "Vice walks through paths full of present lusts and persuades many to follow it. Virtue pursues a steep path and is less seductive to mankind, especially if at another place there are persons who call them to a gently declining road."

(Diary, 1815.)

275. "Sensual enjoyment without a union of soul is bestial and will always remain bestial."

(Diary, 1812–18.)

276. "Men are not only together when they are with each other; even the distant and the dead live with us."

(To Therese Malfatti, later Baroness von Drossdick, to whom in the country he sent Goethe's "Wilhelm Meister" and Schlegel's translation of Shakespeare.)

277. "There is no goodness except the possession of a good soul, which may be seen in all things, from which one need not seek to hide."

(August 15, 1812, to Bettina von Arnim.)

278. "The foundation of friendship demands the greatest likeness of human souls and hearts."

(Baden, July 24, 1804, to Ries, describing his quarrel with Breuning.)

279. "True friendship can rest only on the union of like natures."

(Diary, 1812–18.)

280. "The people say nothing; they are merely people. As a rule they only see themselves in others, and what they see is nothing; away with them! The good and the beautiful needs no people,—it exists without outward help, and this seems to be the reason of our enduring friendship."

(September 16, 1812, to Amalie Sebald, in Teplitz, who had playfully called him a tyrant.)

281. "Look, my dear Ries; these are the great connoisseurs who affect to be able to judge of any piece of music so correctly and keenly. Give them but the name of their favorite,—they need no more!"

(To his pupil Ries, who had, as a joke, played a mediocre march at a gathering at Count Browne's and announced it to be a composition by Beethoven. When the march was praised beyond measure Beethoven broke out into a grim laugh.)

282. "Do not let all men see the contempt which they deserve; we do not know when we may need them."

(Note in the Diary of 1814, after having had an unpleasant experience with his "friend" Bertolini. "Henceforth never step inside his house; shame on you to ask anything from such an one.")

283. "Our Time stands in need of powerful minds who will scourge these petty, malicious and miserable scoundrels,—much as my heart resents doing injury to a fellow man."

(In 1825, to his nephew, in reference to the publication of a satirical canon on the Viennese publisher, Haslinger, by Schott, of Mayence.)

284. "Today is Sunday. Shall I read something for you from the Gospels? 'Love ye one another!'"

(To Frau Streicher.)

285. "Hate reacts on those who nourish it."
(Diary, 1812–18.)

286. "When friends get into a quarrel it is always best not to call in an intermediary, but to have friend turn to friend direct."
(Vienna, November 2, 1793, to Eleonore von Breuning, of Bonn.)

287. "There are reasons for the conduct of men which one is not always willing to explain, but which, nevertheless, are based on ineradicable necessity."
(In 1815, to Brauchle.)

288. "I was formerly inconsiderate and hasty in the expression of my opinions, and thereby I made enemies. Now I pass judgment on no one, and, indeed, for the reason that I do not wish to do any one harm. Moreover, in the last instance I always think: if it is something decent it will maintain itself in spite of all attack and envy; if there is nothing good and sound at the bottom of it, it will fall to pieces of itself, bolster it up as one may."
(In a conversation with Tomaschek, in October, 1814.)

289. "Even the most sacred friendship may harbor secrets, but you ought not to misinterpret the secret of a friend because you can not guess it."
(About 1808, to Frau Marie Bigot.)

290. "You are happy; it is my wish that you remain so, for every man is best placed in his sphere."
(Bonn, July 13, 1825, to his brother Johann, landowner in Gneisendorf.)

291. "One must not measure the cost of the useful."
(To his nephew Karl in a discussion touching the purchase of an expensive book.)

292. "It is not my custom to prattle away my purposes, since every intention once betrayed is no longer one's own."
(To Frau Streicher.)

293. "How stupidity and wretchedness always go in pairs!"
(Diary, 1817.)
[Beethoven was greatly vexed by his servants.]

294. "Hope nourishes me; it nourishes half the world, and has been my neighbor all my life, else what had become of me!"
(August 11, 1810, to Bettina von Arnim.)

295. "Fortune is round like a globe, hence, naturally, does not always fall on the noblest and best."
(Vienna, July 29, 1800, to Wegeler.)

296. "Show your power, Fate! We are not our own masters; what is decided must be,—and so be it!"

(Diary, 1818.)

297. "Eternal Providence omnisciently directs the good and evil fortunes of mortal men."

(Diary, 1818.)

298. "With tranquility, O God, will I submit myself to changes, and place all my trust in Thy unalterable mercy and goodness."

(Diary, 1818.)

299. "All misfortune is mysterious and greatest when viewed alone; discussed with others it seems more endurable because one becomes entirely familiar with the things one dreads, and feels as if one had overcome it."

(Diary, 1816.)

300. "One must not flee for protection to poverty against the loss of riches, nor to a lack of friendship against the loss of friends, nor by abstention from procreation against the death of children, but to reason against everything."

(Diary, 1816.)

301. "I share deeply with you the righteous sorrow over the death of your wife. It seems to me that such a parting, which confronts nearly every married man, ought to keep one in the ranks of the unmarried."

(May 20, 1811, to Gottfried Hartel, of Leipzig.)

302. "He who is afflicted with a malady which he can not alter, but which gradually brings him nearer and nearer to death, without which he would have lived longer, ought to reflect that murder or another cause might have killed him even more quickly."

(Diary, 1812–18.)

303. "We finite ones with infinite souls are born only for sorrows and joy and it might almost be said that the best of us receive joy through sorrow."

(October 19, 1815, to Countess Erdody.)

304. "He is a base man who does not know how to die; I knew it as a boy of fifteen."

(In the spring of 1816, to Miss Fanny Giannatasio del Rio, when Beethoven felt ill and spoke of dying. It is not known that he was ever near death in his youth.)

305. "A second and third generation recompenses me three and fourfold for the ill-will which I had to endure from my former contemporaries."

(Copied into his Diary from Goethe's "West-ostlicher Divan.")

306. "My hour at last is come; Yet not ingloriously or passively I die, but first will do some valiant deed, Of which mankind shall hear in after time."—Homer.

("The Iliad" [Bryant's translation], Book XXII, 375–378.)

(Copied into his Diary, 1815.)

307. "Fate gave man the courage of endurance."

(Diary, 1814.)

308. "Portia—How far that little candle throws his beams! So shines a good deed in a naughty world."

(Marked in his copy of Shakespeare's "Merchant of Venice.")

309. "And on the day that one becomes a slave, The Thunderer, Jove, takes half his worth away."—Homer.

("The Odyssey" [Bryant's translation], Book XVII, 392–393. Marked by Beethoven.)

310. "Short is the life of man, and whoso bears A cruel heart, devising cruel things, On him men call down evil from the gods While living, and pursue him, when he dies, With scoffs. But whoso is of generous heart And harbors generous aims, his guests proclaim His praises far and wide to all mankind, And numberless are they who call him good."—Homer.

("The Odyssey" [Bryant's translation], Book XIX, 408–415. Copied into his diary, 1818.)

Chapter 13

On God

Beethoven was through and through a religious man, though not in the confessional sense. Reared in the Catholic faith he early attained to an independent opinion on religious things. It must be borne in mind that his youth fell in the period of enlightenment and rationalism. When at a later date he composed the grand Mass in honor of his esteemed pupil Archduke Rudolph,—he hoped to obtain from him a chapelmastership when the Archduke became Archbishop of Olmutz, but in vain,—he gave it forms and dimensions which deviated from the ritual.

In all things liberty was the fundamental principle of Beethoven's life. His favorite book was Sturm's "Observations Concerning God's Works in Nature" (Betrachtungen uber die Werke Gottes in der Natur), which he recommended to the priests for wide distribution among the people. He saw the hand of God in even the most insignificant natural phenomenon. God was to him the Supreme Being whom he had jubilantly hymned in the choral portion of the Ninth Symphony in the words of Schiller: "Brothers, beyond yon starry canopy there must dwell a loving Father!" Beethoven's relationship to God was that of a child toward his loving father to whom he confides all his joys as well as sorrows.

It is said that once he narrowly escaped excommunication for having said that Jesus was only a poor human being and a Jew. Haydn, ingenuously pious, is reported to have called Beethoven an atheist.

He consented to the calling in of a priest on his death-bed. Eye-witnesses testify that the customary function was performed most impressively and edifyingly and that Beethoven expressed his thanks to the officiating priest with heartiness. After he had left the room Beethoven said to his friends: "Plaudite, amici, comoedia finita est," the phrase with which antique dramas were concluded. From this fact the statement has been made that Beethoven wished to characterize the sacrament of extreme unction as a comedy. This is contradicted, however, by his conduct during its administration. It is more probable that he wished to designate his life as a drama; in this sense, at any rate, the words were accepted by his friends. Schindler says emphatically: "The last days were in all respects remarkable, and he looked forward to death with truly Socratic wisdom and peace of mind."

[I append a description of the death scene as I found it in the notebooks of A. W. Thayer which were placed in my hands for examination after the death of Beethoven's greatest biographer in 1897:

"June 5, 1860, I was in Graz and saw Huttenbrenner (Anselm) who gave me the following particulars: . . . In the winter of 1826–27 his friends wrote him from Vienna, that if he wished to see Beethoven again alive he must hurry thither from Graz. He hastened to Vienna, arriving a few days before Beethoven's death. Early in the afternoon of March 26, Huttenbrenner went into the dying man's room. He mentioned as persons whom he saw there, Stephen v. Breuning and Gerhard, Schindler, Telscher and Carl's mother (this seems to be a mistake, i.e. if Mrs. v. Beethoven is right). Beethoven had then long been senseless. Telscher began drawing the dying face of Beethoven. This grated on Breuning's feelings, and he remonstrated with him, and he put up his papers and left (?).

Then Breuning and Schindler left to go out to Wohring to select a grave. (Just after the five—I got this from Breuning himself—when it grew dark with the sudden storm Gerhard, who had been standing at the window, ran home to his teacher.)

Afterward Gerhard v. B. went home, and there remained in the room only Huttenbrenner and Mrs. van Beethoven. The storm passed over, covering the Glacis with snow and sleet. As it passed away a flash of lightning lighted up everything. This was followed by an awful clap of thunder. Huttenbrenner had been sitting on the side of the bed sustaining Beethoven's head—holding it up with his right arm His breathing was already very much impeded, and he had been for hours dying. At this startling, awful peal of thunder, the dying man suddenly raised his head from Huttenbrenner's arm, stretched out his own right arm majestically—like a general giving orders to an army. This was but for an instant; the arm sunk back; he fell back. Beethoven was dead.

"Another talk with Huttenbrenner. It seems that Beethoven was at his last gasp, one eye already closed. At the stroke of lightning and the thunder peal he raised his arm with a doubled-up fist; the expression of his eyes and face was that of one defying death,—a look of defiance and power of resistance.

"He must have had his arm under the pillow. I must ask him.

"I did ask him; he had his arm around B.'s neck." H. E. K.]

311. "I am that which is. I am all that was, that is, and that shall be. No mortal man has ever lifted the veil of me. He is solely of himself, and to this Only One all things owe their existence."

(Beethoven's creed. He had found it in Champollion's "The Paintings of Egypt," where it is set down as an inscription on a temple to the goddess Neith. Beethoven had his copy framed and kept it constantly before him on his writing desk. "The relic was a great treasure in his eyes"—Schindler.)

312. "Wrapped in the shadows of eternal solitude, in the impenetrable darkness of the thicket, impenetrable, immeasurable, unapproachable, formlessly extended. Before spirit was breathed (into things) his spirit was, and his only. As mortal eyes (to compare finite and infinite things) look into a shining mirror."

(Copied, evidently, from an unidentified work, by Beethoven; though possibly original with him.)

313. "It was not the fortuitous meeting of the chordal atoms that made the world; if order and beauty are reflected in the constitution of the universe, then there is a God."

(Diary, 1816.)

314. "He who is above,—O, He is, and without Him there is nothing."

(Diary.)

315. "Go to the devil with your 'gracious Sir!' There is only one who can be called gracious, and that is God."

(About 1824 or 1825, to Rampel, a copyist, who, apparently, had been a little too obsequious in his address to Beethoven. [As is customary among the Viennese to this day. H. E. K.])

316. "What is all this compared with the great Tonemaster above! above! above! and righteously the Most High, whereas here below all is mockery,—dwarfs,—and yet Most High!!"

(To Schott, publisher in Mayence, in 1822—the same year in which Beethoven copied the Egyptian inscription.)

317. "There is no loftier mission than to approach the Divinity nearer than other men, and to disseminate the divine rays among mankind."

(August, 1823, to Archduke Rudolph.)

318. "Heaven rules over the destiny of men and monsters (literally, human and inhuman beings), and so it will guide me, too, to the better things of life."

(September 11, 1811, to the poet Elsie von der Recke.)

319. "It's the same with humanity; here, too (in suffering), he must show his strength, i.e. endure without knowing or feeling his nullity, and reach his perfection again for which the Most High wishes to make us worthy."

(May 13, 1816, to Countess Erdody, who was suffering from incurable lameness.)

320. "Religion and thorough-bass are settled things concerning which there should be no disputing."

(Reported by Schindler.)

331. "All things flowed clear and pure out of God. Though often darkly led to evil by passion, I returned, through penance and purification to the pure fountain,—to God,—and to your art. In this I was never impelled by selfishness; may it always be so. The trees bend low under the weight of fruit, the clouds descend when they are filled with salutary rains, and the benefactors of humanity are not puffed up by their wealth."

(Diary, 1815. The first portion seems to be a quotation, but Beethoven continues after the dash most characteristically in his own words and a change of person.)

322. "God is immaterial, and for this reason transcends every conception. Since He is invisible He can have no form. But from what we observe in His work we may conclude that He is eternal, omnipotent, omniscient and omnipresent."

(Copied, with the remark: "From Indian literature" from an unidentified work, into the Diary of 1816.)

323. "In praise of Thy goodness I must confess that Thou didst try with all Thy means to draw me to Thee. Sometimes it pleased Thee to let me feel the heavy hand of Thy displeasure and to humiliate my proud heart by manifold castigations. Sickness and misfortune didst Thou send upon me to turn my thoughts to my errantries.—One thing, only, O Father, do I ask: cease not to labor for my betterment. In whatsoever manner it be, let me turn to Thee and become fruitful in good works."

(Copied into the Diary from Sturm's book, "Observations Concerning the Works of God in Nature.")

Appendix

Some observations may finally be acceptable touching Beethoven's general culture to which the thoughts of the reader must naturally have been directed by the excerpts from his writings set forth in the preceding pages. His own words betray the fact that he was not privileged to enjoy a thorough school-training and was thus compelled to the end of his days to make good the deficiencies in his learning. As a lad at Bonn he had attended the so-called Tirocinium, a sort of preparatory school for the Gymnasium, and acquired a small knowledge of Latin. Later he made great efforts to acquire French, a language essential to intercourse in the upper circles of society. He never established intimate relations with the rules of German. He used small initials for substantives, or capitalized verbs and adjectives according as they appeared important to him. His punctuation was arbitrary; generally he drew a perpendicular line between his words, letting it suffice for a comma or period as the case might be (a proceeding which adds not a little to the embarrassments of him who seeks to translate his sometimes mystical utterances).

It is said that a man's bookcase bears evidence of his education and intellectual interests. Beethoven also had books,—not many, but a characteristic collection. From his faithful friend and voluntary servant Schindler we have a report on this subject. Of the books of which he was possessed at the time of his death there have been preserved four volumes of translations of Shakespeare's works, Homer's "Odyssey" in the translation of J. H. Voss, Sturm's "Observations" (several times referred to in the preceding pages), and Goethe's "West-ostlicher Divan." These books are frequently marked and annotated in lead pencil, thus bearing witness to the subjects which interested Beethoven. From them, and volumes which he had borrowed, many passages were copied by him into his daily journal. Besides these books Schindler mentions Homer's "Iliad," Goethe's poems, "Wilhelm Meister" and "Faust," Schiller's dramas and poems, Tiedge's "Urania," volumes of poems by Matthisson and Seume, and Nina d'Aubigny's "Letters to Natalia on Singing,"—a book to which Beethoven attached great value.

These books have disappeared, as well as others which Beethoven valued. We do not know what became of the volumes of Plato, Aristotle, Plutarch and Xenophon, or the writings of Pliny, Euripides, Quintilian, Ovid, Horace, Ossian, Milton and Thomson, traces of which are found in Beethoven's utterances.

The catalogue made for the auction sale of his posthumous effects on September 7, 1827, included forty-four works of which the censorship seized five as prohibited writings, namely, Seume's "Foot Journey to Syracuse," the Apocrypha, Kotzebue's "On the Nobility," W.E. Muller's "Paris in its Zenith" (1816), and "Views on Religion and Ecclesiasticism." Burney's "General History of Music" was also in his library, the gift, probably of an English admirer.

In his later years Beethoven was obliged to use the oft-quoted "conversation-books" in his intercourse with friends and strangers alike who wrote down their questions. Of these little books Schindler preserved no less than 134, which are now in the Royal Library in Berlin. Naturally Beethoven answered the written questions orally as a rule. An idea of Beethoven's opinions can occasionally be gathered from the context of the questions, but frequently we are left in the dark.

Beethoven's own characterization of his deafness as "singular" is significant. Often, even in his later years, he was able to hear a little and for a time. One might almost speak of a periodical visitation of the "demon." In his biography Marx gives the following description of the malady: "As early as 1816 it is found that he is incapable of conducting his own works; in 1824 he could not hear the storm of applause from a great audience; but in 1822 he still improvises marvelously in social circles; in 1826 he studies their parts in the Ninth Symphony and Solemn Mass with Sontag and Ungher, and in 1825 he listens critically to a performance of the quartet in A-minor, op. 132."

It is to be assumed that in such urgent cases his willpower temporarily gave new tension to the gradually atrophying aural nerves (it is said that he was still able to hear single or a few voices with his left ear but could not apprehend masses), but this was not the case in less important moments, as the conversation-books prove. In these books a few answers are also written down, naturally enough in cases not intended for the ears of strangers. At various times Beethoven kept a diary in which he entered his most intimate thoughts, especially those designed for his own encouragement. Many of these appear in the preceding pages. In these instances more than in any others his expressions are obscure, detached and, through indifference, faulty in construction. For the greater part they are remarks thrown upon the paper in great haste.

www.ingramcontent.com/pod-product-compliance
Lightning Source LLC
Chambersburg PA
CBHW022125280326
41933CB00007B/554